Minot Judson Savage

Sacred songs for public worship

A hymn and tune book

Minot Judson Savage

Sacred songs for public worship
A hymn and tune book

ISBN/EAN: 9783337266196

Printed in Europe, USA, Canada, Australia, Japan

Cover: Foto ©Thomas Meinert / pixelio.de

More available books at **www.hansebooks.com**

SACRED SONGS FOR PUBLIC WORSHIP

A Hymn and Tune Book

EDITED BY

M. J. SAVAGE AND HOWARD M. DOW

——— — —

BOSTON

GEO. H. ELLIS, 272 CONGRESS STREET

1899

PREFACE

So MANY Hymn and Tune Books are already before the public that perhaps one may be fairly expected to apologize for adding another to the growing list. The editor's original intention, as in the case of his *Hand Book*, was simply to prepare something for his own personal use. But this second venture, like the first, has grown beyond the original purpose. Under the urgency of the Standing Committee of his own church, and of representatives of other churches, who thought they also might care to use it, the editor has gone on to the completion of what is now offered to the public.

If anybody, besides the editor, shall care to adopt it, it must be because they are in substantial agreement with him as to what is desirable in a collection of hymns and tunes for the ordinary uses of Sunday worship. It is fitting then that he should briefly indicate the principles by which he has been guided.

1. It was determined that the book should be small. In eight years' ministry with the Church of the Unity, it was found that less than sixty hymns of the American Unitarian Association collection had been used. There seemed no adequate reason for continuing to pick those less than sixty out of a collection of eight hundred.

2. The editor desired, for his own use, hymns touching on some new topics, and many old topics in new ways, such as he did not find in any one previous collection. He has attempted to meet this want by selections from many various sources, and by considerable original contributions of his own. He does not claim any complete success in this

direction; nor does he mean to set up his book as a standard by which others are to be criticised or condemned. He does hope, however, to supply his own want better in this way.

3. As to music, it was determined that every tune should be familiar. Whatever may be possible in some cases, it is generally found to be impracticable to get congregations to practise and learn new music. But, however often it is sung, people will always greet a familiar tune with all the enthusiasm of old acquaintance. They thus join heartily in the service. And so the one end of congregational singing is attained. Enough variety may always be secured through the contributions of the choir.

The test of familiarity, then, has been rigidly applied, with the exception of a few original pieces written to accompany some special original songs.

4. It was found that a topical arrangement of the hymns would necessitate their separation from the tunes with which it was thought best to wed them. It was determined, therefore, that convenience for singing should take precedence. The order of the hymns then has been determined by the music; and so, in every case, the hymn and its tune will be found at the same opening.

But the topical index of first lines will make it very easy to find any hymn, on any subject, that the book contains.

5. The editor was urged, by some advisers, to include in his book some forms of congregational service. But it is his opinion that these, when desired, may be as conveniently comprised in a volume by themselves.

6. It seems desirable that a word should be said concerning the doctrinal implications of hymns. It is said that, on a certain occasion, Dr. Bellows was with an English gentleman at a service in King's Chapel. After looking over the revised Service Book, the Englishman, turning to the doctor, remarked, "Ah, I see you Unitarians use the

Prayer Book, *diluted.*" Dr. Bellows replied, "Oh, no! not *diluted; washed!*"

The editor ventures to suggest that our Unitarian Hymn Books have not usually been *washed* enough. He would also say, in all humility, that, in making up this book, he has tried to be always mindful of an ancient command, apparently many times overlooked, — " *Thou shalt worship the Lord thy God, and him only shalt thou serve.*" With all his reverence for Jesus, he cannot think that either good logic or true piety can permit a consistent Unitarian to offer to the Man of Nazareth that worship — either prayer or hymn — which he himself always taught his disciples, both by precept and example, should be given to God alone.

7. If any one should think that the editor has included too large a proportion of his own composition, he stands ready with a threefold reply : —

(1) He pleads guilty.

(2) He suggests his original intention,— to make a book merely for his own use.

(3) He would remind the objector that enough for all practical purposes may be found, though all of his own composition are passed by.

M. J. S.

CONTENTS.

INDEX OF SUBJECTS.

(vii)

INDEX OF SUBJECTS

INDEX OF SUBJECTS

CLASSIFIED INDEX.

(Arranged by First Lines.)

I. LIFE.

II. SORROW AND HOPE.

III. TIMES.

IV. WORSHIP.

INDEX OF FIRST LINES.

(xiii)

INDEX OF FIRST LINES

INDEX OF FIRST LINES

(xv)

INDEX TO TUNES.

(xvi)

INDEX OF METRES.

INDEX OF AUTHORS.

MISSIONARY CHANT L. M.

I *Hymn of Autumn*

O LORD of seasons! unto thee
Our hymn with grateful heart we raise
For all thy gifts, so rich and free,
That crown these sweet autumnal days.

By thy dear love, the lap of spring
Was heaped with many a blooming
    flower,
And smiling summer joyed to bring
The sunshine and the gentle shower.

And autumn pours her riches now
Of ripening grain and bursting shell ;
And golden sheaf and laden bough
The fulness of thy bounty tell.

Beneath blue skies, the fragrant breeze
O'er rustling, fallen leaves doth blow ;
In gold and purple robed, the trees
The fulness of thy beauty show.

Anon

2 *A Harvest Song*

ONCE more the liberal year laughs out
O'er richer stores than gems or gold ;
Once more with harvest-song and shout
Is Nature's bloodless triumph told.

O favors every year made new !
O blessings with the sunshine sent !
The bounty overruns our due ;
The fulness shames our discontent.

We shut our eyes, the flowers bloom on ;
We murmur, but the corn-ears fill ;
We choose the shadow, but the sun
That casts it shines behind us still.

Now let these altars, wreathed with
    flowers
And piled with fruits, awake again
Thanksgiving for the golden hours,
The early and the latter rain !

J. G. Whittier

7

FEDERAL STREET L. M.

3 *Organizing a Church*

WHAT purpose burns within our hearts
That we together here should stand,
Pledging each other mutual vows,
And ready hand to join in hand?

We see in vision fair a time
When evil shall have passed away;
And thus we dedicate our lives
To hasten on that blessed day; —

To seek the truth whate'er it be,
To follow it where'er it leads,
To turn to facts our dreams of good,
And coin our lives in loving deeds.

For this, we organize to-day;
To such a church of God we bring
Our utmost love and loyalty,
And make our souls an offering.

M. J. S.

4 *Faith above Creed*

THE waves unbuild the wasting shore;
Where mountains towered, the billows
sweep,
Yet still their borrowed spoils restore,
And raise new empires from the deep.

So, while the floods of thought lay waste
The old domain of chartered creeds,
Its heaven-appointed tides will haste
To shape new homes for human needs.

Be ours to mark with hearts unchilled
The change an outworn age deplores;
The legend sinks, but faith shall build
A fairer throne on new-found shores.

The star shall glow in western skies
That shone o'er Bethlehem's hallowed
shrine,
And once again the temple rise
That crowned the rock of Palestine.

Not when the wondering shepherds
bowed
Did angels sing their latest song,
Nor yet to Israel's kneeling crowd
Did heaven's one sacred dome belong.

Let priest and prophet have their
dues,—
The Levite counts but half a man,
Whose proud salvation of the Jews
Shuts out the Good Samaritan!

8

Though scattered far, the flock may
    stray:
His own the Shepherd still shall claim,—
The saints who never learned to pray,
The friends who never spoke his name.

Dear Master, while we hear thy voice
That says, "The truth shall make you
    free,"
Thy servants still by loving choice,
Oh, keep us faithful unto thee!

                 Oliver Wendell Holmes

5   *Ordaining a Minister*

Who is he fit to teach and guide
Those who are seeking out the way
That, through the darkness of their life,
Leads up to God's eternal day?

He who with loyalty to truth
When she moves forward turns not back;
Who shrinks not though the way be hard,
And shapes of danger throng his track;

Whose heart with tenderness can melt;
Who knows the weaknesses of men;
Who will not quench the smoking flax,
But kindle to a flame again;

He who is patient of delay:
Who knoweth both to work and wait,
That God's time never comes too soon,
And, while he waits, 'tis never late.

                         M. J. S.

6   *The Advancing God*

In darker days and nights of storm,
Men knew God but to fear his form;
And in the reddest lightnings saw
His arm avenge insulted law.

In brighter days, we read his love
In flowers beneath, in stars above;
And in the track of every storm
Behold his cheering rainbow form.

E'en in the reddest lightning's path,
We see no vestiges of wrath;
But always wisdom, perfect love,
From flowers below to stars above.

See, from on high sweet influence rains
On palace, cottage, mountains, plains!
No hour of wrath shall mortals fear,
While true parental love is here.

                     Theodore Parker

7   *God is Good*

Our God is good: in earth and sky,
From ocean-depths and spreading wood,
Ten thousand voices seem to cry,
"God made us all, and God is good."

The sun that keeps his trackless way,
And downward pours his golden flood,
Night's sparkling hosts, all seem to say,
In accents clear, that God is good.

I hear it in the rushing breeze:
The hills that have for ages stood,
The echoing sky and roaring seas,
All swell the chorus, "God is good."

Yea, God is good, all nature says,
By God's own hand with speech endued;
And man, in louder notes of praise,
Should sing for joy that God is good.

                 John Hampden Gurney

DUKE STREET L. M.

8 *God with Us*

O GOD, whose presence glows in all
Within, around us, and above!
Thy word we bless, thy name we call,
Whose word is Truth, whose name is
　　Love.

That truth be with the heart believed
Of all who seek this sacred place;
With power proclaimed, in peace re-
　　ceived,—
Our spirit's light, thy spirit's grace.

That love its holy influence pour,
To keep us meek and make us free,
And throw its binding blessing more
Round each with all, and all with thee.

Send down its angel to our side,
Send in its calm upon the breast;
For we would know no other guide,
And we can need no other rest.

N. L. Frothingham

9 *God Incomprehensible*

GREAT GOD, in vain man's narrow view
Attempts to look thy nature through:
Our laboring powers with reverence own
Thy glories never can be known.

Not the high seraph's mighty thought,
Who countless years his God has sought,
Such wondrous height or depth can find,
Or fully trace thy boundless mind.

And yet, thy kindness deigns to show
Enough for mortal minds to know;
While wisdom, goodness, power divine
Through all thy works and conduct
　　shine.

Oh, may our souls with rapture trace
Thy works of nature and of grace,
Explore thy sacred truth, and still
Press on to know and do thy will!

Kippis

10

10 *Natural Religion*

WHERE ancient forests widely spread,
Where bends the cataract's ocean-fall,
On the lone mountain's silent head,
There are thy temples, God of all!

Beneath the dark blue midnight arch,
Whence myriad suns pour down their
rays,   [march,
Where planets trace their ceaseless
Father! we worship as we gaze.

All space is holy, for all space
Is filled by thee; but human thought
Burns clearer in some chosen place
Where thy own works of love are taught.

Here be they taught! and may we know
That trust thy servants knew of old,
Which onward bears through weal or
woe,
Till deeper, fuller life unfold.
A. Norton

11 *The Presence*

MYSTERIOUS Presence, Source of all,—
The world without, the soul within,—
Fountain of Life, oh, hear our call,
And pour thy living waters in!

Thou breathest in the rushing wind,
Thy spirit stirs in leaf and flower;
Nor wilt thou from the willing mind
Withhold thy light and love and power.

Thy hand unseen to accents clear
Awoke the Psalmist's trembling lyre,
And touched the lips of holy seer
With flame from thine own altar-fire.

That touch divine still, Lord, impart;
Still give the prophet's burning word;
And vocal in each waiting heart
Let living psalms of praise be heard.
S. C. Beach

12 *Another Day*

O GOD, I thank thee for each sight
Of beauty that thy hand doth give,—
For sunny skies and air and light;
O God, I thank thee that I live!

That life I consecrate to thee;
And ever, as the day is born,
On wings of joy my soul would flee,
And thank thee for another morn,—

Another day in which to cast
Some silent deed of love abroad,
That, greatening as it journeys past,
May do some earnest work for God;

Another day to do, to dare,
To tax anew my growing strength,
To arm my soul with faith and prayer,
And so reach heaven and thee at length.
Mrs. C. A. Mason

13 *Retirement and Meditation*

MY God, permit me not to be
A stranger to myself and thee:
Amidst a thousand thoughts I rove,
Forgetful of my highest love.

Why should my passions mix with earth,
And thus debase my heavenly birth?
Why should I cleave to things below,
And [thus my nobler life forego]?

Call me away from flesh and sense,—
One sovereign word can draw me thence:
I would obey the voice divine,
And all inferior joys resign.

Be earth, with all her scenes, withdrawn;
Let noise and vanity be gone.
In secret silence of the mind,
My heaven, and there my God, I find.
Watts

11

HEBRON I. M.

14 *The House of God*

Lo, God is here! let us adore
And humbly bow before his face;
Let all within us feel his power,
Let all within us seek his grace.

Lo, God is here! him day and night
United choirs of angels sing;
To him, enthroned above all height,
Heaven's host their noblest homage
 bring.

Being of beings! may our praise
Thy courts with grateful fragrance fill;
Still may we stand before thy face,
Still hear and do thy sovereign will.
Salisbury Coll.

15 *The Sacrifice of the Heart*

When, as returns this solemn day,
Man comes to meet his Maker, God,
What rites, what honors, shall he pay?
How spread his Sovereign's praise
 abroad?

From marble domes and gilded spires
Shall curling clouds of incense rise,
And gems and gold and garlands deck
The costly pomp of sacrifice?

Vain, sinful man! creation's Lord
Thy golden offerings well may spare;
But give thy heart, and thou shalt find
Here dwells a God who heareth prayer.
Mrs. Barbauld

16 *Eternity of God*

Ere mountains reared their forms sub-
 lime,
Or heaven and earth in order stood;
Before the birth of ancient time;
From everlasting,—thou art God.

A thousand ages in their flight
With thee are as a fleeting day:
Past, present, future, to thy sight
At once their various scenes display.

But our brief life's a shadowy dream,
A passing thought that soon is o'er,
That fades with morning's earliest
 beam,
And fills the musing mind no more.

To us, O Lord! the wisdom give
Each passing moment so to spend
That we at length with thee may live
Where life and bliss shall never end.
Spirit of the Psalms

12

MAY I resolve with all my heart,
With all my powers to serve the Lord;
Nor from his precepts e'er depart,
Whose service is a rich reward!

Be this the purpose of the soul,
My solemn, my determined choice,—
To yield to his supreme control,
And in his kind commands rejoice.

Oh, may I never faint nor tire,
Nor, wandering, leave his sacred ways!
Great God, accept my soul's desire,
And give me strength to live thy praise.
Anne Steele

18   *God ever Near*

WHAT secret place, what distant star,
O Lord of all, is thine abode?
Why dwellest thou from us so far?
We yearn for thee, thou hidden God.

And not in vain we seek, we yearn;
We need not stretch our weary wings:
Thou meetest us where'er we turn;
Thou dwellest, Lord, within all things.

O Glory that no eye can bear!
O Presence bright, our inward guest!
O farthest off, most closely near,
Most hidden and most manifest!

No need, in search of thine abode,
Through starry spheres our thoughts
        should roam,
Thou, Holy Spirit, mighty God,
Dost make in human hearts thy home!
T. H. Gill

MY gracious God, I own thy right
To every service I can pay;
And call it my supreme delight
To hear thy dictates, and obey.

What is my being but for thee,
Its sure support, its noblest end,—
Thy ever smiling face to see,
And serve the cause of such a friend?

Thy work my feeble age shall bless,
When youthful vigor is no more;
And my last hour of life confess
Thy love hath animating power.
Doddridge

20   *Wisdom and Virtue sought from God*

ASSIST us, Lord, to act, to be
What nature and thy laws decree,
Worthy that intellectual flame
Which from thy breathing Spirit came.

Our moral freedom to maintain,
Bid passion serve and reason reign,
Self-poised, and independent still
On this world's varying good or ill.

May our expanded souls disclaim
The narrow view, the selfish aim;
But with a [world-wide love] embrace
Whate'er is friendly to our race.

O Father! grace and virtue grant;
No more we wish, no more we want:
To know, to serve thee, and to love,
Is peace below,— is bliss above.
Henry Moore

HAMBURG L. M.

21 *A Prayer for Faith*

I ask not wealth, but power to take
And use the things I have aright ;
Not years, but wisdom that shall make
My life a profit and delight.

I ask not that for me the plan
Of good and ill be set aside,
But that the common lot of man
Be nobly borne and glorified.

I know I may not always keep
My steps in places green and sweet,
Nor find the pathway of the deep
A path of safety to my feet ;

But pray that, when the tempest's breath
Shall fiercely sweep my way about,
I make not shipwreck of my faith
In the unfathomed sea of doubt.

Elim

22 *The Hope of Man*

The past is dark with sin and shame,
The future dim with doubt and fear ;
But, Father, yet we praise thy name,
Whose guardian love is always near.

For man has striven, ages long,
With faltering steps to come to thee ;
And, in each purpose high and strong,
The influence of thy grace could see.

He could not breathe an earnest prayer,
But thou wast kinder than he dreamed,
As age by age brought hopes more fair,
And nearer still thy kingdom seemed.

But never rose within his breast
A trust so calm and deep as now :
Shall not the weary find a rest?
Father, Preserver, answer thou !

T. W. Higginson

14

23
An Independent and Happy Life

How HAPPY is he, born or taught,
Who serveth not another's will;
Whose armor is his honest thought,
And simple truth his highest skill;

Whose passions not his masters are;
Whose soul is still prepared for death,
Not tied unto the world with care
Of prince's ear or vulgar breath;

Who God doth late and early pray
More of his grace than goods to lend;
And walks with man, from day to day,
As with a brother and a friend,—

This man is freed from servile bands
Of hope to rise or fear to fall;
Lord of himself, though not of lands,
And, having nothing, yet hath all.

Sir Henry Wotton

24
Winter

'Tis winter now; the fallen snow
Has left the heavens all coldly clear;
Through leafless boughs the sharp winds
blow,
And all the earth lies dead and drear.

And yet God's love is not withdrawn;
His life within the keen air breathes,
His beauty paints the crimson dawn
And clothes the boughs with glittering
wreaths.

And tho' abroad the sharp winds blow,
And skies are chill and frosts are keen,
Home closer draws her circle now,
And warmer glows her light within.

O God, who giv'st the winter's cold
As well as summer's joyous rays,
Us warmly in thy love enfold,
And keep us through life's wintry days.

S. Longfellow

25
The Mother's Hymn

LORD, who ordainest for mankind
Benignant toils and tender cares,
We thank thee for the ties that bind
The mother to the child she bears.

We thank thee for the hopes that rise
Within her heart as, day by day,
The dawning soul from those young eyes
Looks with a clearer, steadier ray.

And, grateful for the blessing given,
With that dear infant on her knee,
She trains the eye to look to heaven,
The voice to lisp a prayer to thee.

All-gracious! grant to those who bear
A mother's charge the strength and light
To guide the feet that own their care
In ways of love and truth and right.

Bryant

26
Vesper Hymn

AGAIN, as evening's shadow falls,
We gather in these hallowed walls;
And vesper hymn and vesper prayer
Rise mingling on the holy air.

May struggling hearts that seek release
Here find the rest of God's own peace;
And, strengthened here by hymn and
prayer,
Lay down the burden and the care!

O God, our light! to thee we bow;
Within all shadows standest thou:
Give deeper calm than night can bring,
Give sweeter songs than lips can sing.

Life's tumult we must meet again;
We cannot at the shrine remain;
But, in the spirit's secret cell,
May hymn and prayer forever dwell!

S. Longfellow

ALL SAINTS L. M.

27 *Greeting*

O LIFE that maketh all things new,—
The blooming earth, the thoughts of
    men!
Our pilgrim feet, wet with thy dew,
In gladness hither turn again.

From hand to hand the greeting flows,
From eye to eye the signals run,
From heart to heart the bright hope
    glows:
The seekers of the Light are one,—

One in the freedom of the truth,
One in the joy of paths untrod,
One in the soul's perennial youth,
One in the larger thought of God,—

The freer step, the fuller breath,
The wide horizon's grander view,
The sense of life that knows no death,
The Life that maketh all things new.
              S. Longfellow

28 *The Love of God*

O SOURCE divine and Life of all,
The Fount of being's wondrous sea!
Thy depth would every heart appall
That saw not love supreme in thee.

We shrink before thy vast abyss,
Where worlds on worlds unnumbered
    brood:
We know thee truly but in this,—
That thou bestowest all our good.

And so, 'mid boundless time and space,
Oh, grant us still in thee to dwell,
And through the ceaseless web to trace
Thy presence working all things well!

Bestow on every joyous thrill
A deeper tone of reverent awe;
Make pure thy children's erring will,
And teach their hearts to love **thy law**
              John Sterling

29 *Life's Meaning*

HE liveth long who liveth well:
All else is being flung away.
He liveth longest who can tell
Of true things truly done each day.

Be wise, and use thy wisdom well:
Who wisdom speaks must live it, too.
He is the wisest who can tell
How first he lived, then spake, the true.

Sow truth, if thou the true would'st
reap:
Who sows the false shall reap the vain;
Erect and sound thy conscience keep;
From hollow words and deeds refrain.

Sow love, and taste its fruitage pure;
Sow peace, and reap its harvest bright;
Sow sunbeams on the rock and moor,
And find a harvest home of light.

Bonar

30 *Consecration of Children*

THE very blossoms of our life,
The treasures that no wealth could buy,
We freely bring them here to-day
And give them up to thee, Most High.

Not, as in olden times, to death,
To hermit life, or darksome days;
But unto beauty, goodness, truth,
To all high thoughts and noble ways.

To find and serve thee in the world,
By seeking truth and helping men,—
To this we consecrate them now,
And day by day will o'er again.

Thus do we keep them while we give,
And make them still of nobler worth.
When all the world is given thus,
Heav'n will indeed have come on earth.
M. J. S.

31 *Not Afar Off*

WHEN up to nightly skies we gaze,
Where stars pursue their endless ways,
We think we see from earth's low clod
The wide and shining home of God.

But, could we rise to moon or sun,
Or path where planets duly run,
Still, heaven would spread above us far,
And earth remote would seem a star.

This earth, with all its dust and tears,
Is his, no less than yonder spheres;
And rain-drops weak and grains of sand
Are stamped by his immediate hand.

The rock, the wave, the little flower,—
All fed by streams of living power
That spring from one almighty will,—
Whate'er his thought conceives fulfil.

We view those halls of painted air,
And own thy presence makes them fair;
But nearer still to thee, O Lord,
Is he whose thoughts with thine accord.
Sterling

17

WARD L. M.

32 *" Why seek ye the Living among the Dead "*

Ah! why should bitter tears be shed
In sorrow o'er the mounded sod,
When verily there are no dead
Of all the children of our God?

They who are lost to outward sense
Have but flung off their robes of clay,
And, clothed in heavenly radiance,
Attend us on our lowly way.

And oft their spirits breathe in ours
The hope and strength and love of theirs,
Which bloom as bloom the early flowers
In breath of summer's viewless airs.

Let living Faith serenely pour
Her sunlight on our pathway dim,
And Death can have no terrors more;
But holy joy shall walk with him.

G. S. Burleigh

33 *Very Near*

Oh, sometimes comes to soul and sense
The feeling which is evidence
That very near about us lies
The realm of spirit-mysteries.

The low and dark horizon lifts,
To light the scenic terror shifts;
The breath of a diviner air
Blows down the answer of a prayer.

Then all our sorrow, pain, and doubt
A great compassion clasps about;
And law and goodness, love and force,
Are wedded fast beyond divorce.

Then, Duty leaves to Love its task,
The beggar Self forgets to ask;
We feel, as flowers the sun and dew,
The One True Life our own renew.

J. G. Whittier

18

ABIDE not in the realm of dreams,
O man, however fair it seems;
But with clear eye the present scan,
And hear the call of God and man.

Think not in sleep to fold thy hands,
Forgetful of thy Lord's commands :
From duty's claims no life is free,—
Behold, to-day hath need of thee!

While the day lingers, do thy best.
Full soon the night will bring its rest ;
And, duty done, that rest shall be
Full of beatitudes to thee.

William H. Burleigh

35   *Heaven*

WHAT is that goal of human hope,
That heaven, where every soul is blest?
'Tis light for those who darkly grope;
To weary ones, 'tis perfect rest ;

To young and eager souls, a place
Where high deeds may be grandly
         wrought ;
To those who mourn some absent face,
'Tis where the lost ones may be sought.

It is a land where each may find
That which in vain he sought for here;
Where every element is kind,
And summer reigns the live-long year.

Is there a country such as this?
Some glad day thou shalt know, O soul!
Hope whispers of the perfect bliss,
And points her finger toward the goal.

M. J. S.

LIKE shadows gliding o'er the plain,
Or clouds that roll successive on,
Man's busy generations pass;   [gone.
And, while we gaze, their forms are

O Father, in whose mighty hand
The boundless years and ages lie,
Teach us thy boon of life to prize,
And use the moments as they fly;

To crowd the narrow span of life
With wise designs and virtuous deeds:
So shall we wake from death's dark night
To share the glory that succeeds.

J. Taylor

37   *The Parting here, the Greeting there*

GOD giveth quietness at last !
The common way once more is passed
From pleading tears and lingerings fond
To fuller life and love beyond.

Fold the rapt soul in your embrace,
Dear ones familiar with the place !
While to the gentle greetings there,
We answer here with murmured prayer.

O silent land to which we move !
Enough if there alone be love,
And mortal need can ne'er outgrow
What it is waiting to bestow !

O pure soul! from that far-off shore
Float some sweet song the waters o'er:
Our faith confirm, our fears dispel,
With the dear voice we loved so well !

John G. Whittier

ERNAN L. M.

38 *Blessed are they that mourn*

DEEM not that they are blest alone,
Whose days a peaceful tenor keep :
The God who loves our race has shown
A blessing for the eyes that weep.

The light of smiles shall fill again
The lids that overflow with tears,
And weary hours of woe and pain
Are earnests of serener years.

Oh, there are days of hope and rest
For every dark and troubled night!
And grief may bide, an evening guest;
But joy shall come with early light.

And thou who o'er thy friend's low bier
Dost shed the bitter drops like rain,
Hope that a brighter, happier sphere
Will give him to thy arms again.

Bryant

39 *The Better Land*

THERE is a land mine eye hath seen
In visions of enraptured thought,
So bright that all which spreads between
Is with its radiant glory fraught ;

A land upon whose blissful shore
There rests no shadow, falls no stain ;
There those who meet shall part no
more,
And those long parted meet again.

Its skies are not like earthly skies,
With varying hues of shade and light :
It hath no need of suns to rise,
To dissipate the gloom of night.

There sweeps no desolating wind
Across that calm, serene abode :
The wanderer there a home may find
Within the paradise of God.

Anon

20

40 *The Seed*

Now is the seed-time; God alone,
Beyond our vision weak and dim,
Beholds the end of what is sown:
The harvest-time is hid with him.

Yet unforgotten where it lies,
Though seeming on the desert cast,
The seed of gen'rous sacrifice
Shall rise with bloom and fruit, at last.

And he who blesses most is blest;
For God and man shall own his worth
Who toils to leave as his bequest
An added beauty on the earth.
J. G. Whittier

41 *The Righteous blessed in Death*

How BLESSED the righteous when he
dies!
When sinks a weary soul to rest,
How mildly beam the closing eyes,
How gently heaves the expiring breast!

So fades a summer cloud away,
So sinks the gale when storms are o'er,
So gently shuts the eye of day,
So dies a wave along the shore.

A holy quiet reigns around,
A calm which life nor death destroys.
Nothing disturbs that peace profound
Which his unfettered soul enjoys.

Farewell, conflicting hopes and fears,
Where lights and shades alternate dwell:
How bright th' unchanging morn ap-
pears!
Farewell, inconstant world, farewell.

Life's duty done, as sinks the clay,
Light from its load the spirit flies;
While heaven and earth combine to say,
"How blessed the righteous when he
dies!"
Mrs. Barbauld

42 *The Beauty of the World.*

THEY call the world a dreary place,
And tell long tales of sin and woe,
As if there were no blessed trace
Of sunshine to be found below.

They point, when autumn winds
[wail by],
To falling leaves and withered flowers;
But shall we mourn them [when they
die],
And never note their brilliant hours?

They mark the rainbow's fading light,
And say it is the type of man,—
"So passeth he"; but, oh, how bright
The transient glory of the span!

They liken life unto the stream
That swift and shallow pours along;
But beauty marks the rippling gleam,
And music fills the bubbling song.

Oh, why should our own hands [thus
twine]
Dark chaplets from the cypress tree?
Why in each gloomy spot repine,
When further on sweet buds may be?
Eliza Cook

21

OLD HUNDRED L. M

43 *Doxology*

Now, as the parting hour is nigh,
In our last song, with glad refrain,
To God on earth and in the sky
We lift both voice and heart again.

Soon may that blessed morn arise
When, o'er the earth, from east to west,
Thy light shall flood the earth and skies,
And all mankind in thee be blest!

M. J. S.

44 *Doxology*

Be thou, O God, exalted high;
And, as thy glory fills the sky,
So let it be on earth displayed,
Till thou art here, as there, obeyed.

Guillaume Franck

45 *Praise*

From all that dwell below the skies,
Let the Creator's praise arise;
Let [love and righteousness] be sung
Through every land by every tongue.

Eternal are thy mercies, Lord;
Eternal truth attends thy word:
Thy praise shall sound from shore to
shore,
Till suns shall rise and set no more.

Watts

46 *The Opening Year*

Great God, we sing that mighty hand
By which supported still we stand:
The opening year thy mercy shows;
Thy mercy crown it till it close!

By day, by night, at home, abroad,
Still we are guarded by our God;
By his incessant bounty fed,
By his unerring counsel led.

With grateful hearts the past we own;
The future, all to us unknown,
We to thy guardian care commit,
And peaceful leave before thy feet.

In scenes exalted or depressed,
Be thou our joy and thou our rest:
Thy goodness all our hopes shall raise,
Adored through all our changing days.

Doddridge

47   *The Law of Love*

MAKE channels for the streams of love,
  Where they may broadly run;
And love has overflowing founts
  To fill them every one.

But if, at any time, we cease
  Such channels to provide,
The very founts of love for us
  Will soon be parched and dried.

For we must share, if we would keep,
  That blessing from above:
Ceasing to give, we cease to have,—
  Such is the law of love.
                 R. C. Trench

48   *Working with God*

WORKMAN of God, oh, lose not heart,
  But learn what God is like!
And, in the darkest battle-field,
  Thou shalt know where to strike.

Oh, blest is he who can divine
  Where real right doth lie,
And dares to take the side that seems
  Wrong to man's blindfold eye.

Oh, learn to scorn the praise of men!
  Oh, learn to lose with God!
For Jesus won the world through shame,
  And beckons thee his road.
             Frederic W. Faber

49   *The Race of Life*

AWAKE, my soul; stretch every nerve,
  And press with vigor on:
A heavenly race demands thy zeal,
  And an immortal crown.

A cloud of witnesses around
  Hold thee in full survey:
Forget the steps already trod,
  And onward urge thy way.

'Tis God's all-animating voice
  That calls thee from on high;
'Tis his own hand presents the prize
  To thine aspiring eye,—

That prize, with peerless glories bright,
  Which shall new lustre boast
When victors' wreaths and monarchs'
    gems
  Shall blend in common dust.
                Doddridge

HUMMEL C. M.

50 *Receptivity*

Ope, ope, my soul! Around thee press
A thousand things divine:
All glory and all holiness
Are waiting to be thine.

Lie open: Love and Duty stand,
Thy guardian angels, near,
To lead thee gently by the hand,—
Their words of welcome hear.

Lie open, soul: the Beautiful,
That all things doth embrace,
Shall every passion sweetly lull,
And clothe thee in her grace.

Lie open, soul; the great and wise
About thy portal throng;
The wealth of souls before thee lies,
Their gifts to thee belong.

Lie open, soul: in watchfulness
Each brighter glory win;
The Infinite thy peace shall bless,
And God shall enter in.

51 *All Equal before God*

All men are equal in their birth,
Heirs of the earth and skies;
All men are equal when that earth
Fades from their dying eyes.

God meets the throngs who pay their
vows
In courts that hands have made,
And hears the worshipper who bows
Beneath the plantain shade.

'Tis man alone who difference sees,
And speaks of high and low,
And worships those and tramples these,
While the same path they go.

Oh, let man hasten to restore
To all their rights of love!
In power and wealth exult no more,
In wisdom lowly move.

Ye great, renounce your earth-born
pride;
Ye low, your shame and fear:
Live, as ye worship, side by side;
Your brotherhood revere.

H. Martineau

24

52   *Dedication*

O THOU whose own vast temple stands
  Built over earth and sea!
Accept the walls that human hands
  Have raised to worship thee.

Lord, from thine inmost glory send,
  Within these courts to bide,
The peace that dwelleth without end
  Serenely by thy side.

May erring minds that worship here
  Be taught the better way,
And they who mourn, and they who fear,
  Be strengthened as they pray!

May faith grow firm, and love grow
    warm,
  And pure devotion rise,
While round these hallowed walls the
    storm
  Of earth-born passion dies!
                        Bryant

53   *On the Lord's Side*

GOD'S trumpet wakes the slumbering
    world:
  Now, each man to his post!
The red-cross banner is unfurled,—
  Who joins the glorious host?

He who in fealty to the Truth,
  And counting all the cost,
Doth consecrate his gen'rous youth,—
  He joins the noble host!

He who, no anger on his tongue,
  Nor any idle boast,
Bears steadfast witness against wrong,—
  He joins the sacred host!

He who, with calm, undaunted will,
  Ne'er counts the battle lost,
But, though defeated, battles still,—
  He joins the faithful host!

He who is ready for the cross,
  The cause despised loves most,
And shuns not pain, nor shame, nor
    loss,—
  He joins the martyr host!
                        Anon

54   *Be True to Yourself*

BE true to every inmost thought;
  Be as thy thought thy speech;
What thou hast not by suffering bought,
  Presume thou not to teach.

Woe, woe to him, on safety bent,
  Who creeps to age from youth,
Failing to grasp his life's intent,
  Because he fears the truth.

Show forth thy light! If conscience
    gleam,
  Cherish the rising glow:
The smallest spark may shed its beam
  O'er thousand hearts below.

Guard thou the fact, though clouds of
    night
  Down on thy watch-tower stoop,
Though thou shouldst see thine heart's
    delight
  Borne from thee by their swoop.

Face thou the wind, though safer seem
  In shelter to abide.
We were not made to sit and dream:
  The true must first be tried.
                        Alford

25

55 *The Waiting God*

THOU long-disowned, reviled, oppressed
  Strange friend of human kind,
Seeking through weary years a rest
  Within our hearts to find,—

How late thy bright and awful brow
  Breaks through these clouds of sin!
Hail, Truth divine, we know thee now!
  Angel of God, come in!

Come, though with purifying fire
  And desolating sword!
Thou of all nations the desire,
  Earth waits thy cleansing word.

Struck by the lightning of thy glance,
  Let old oppressions die;
Before thy cloudless countenance,
  Let fear and falsehood fly.

Flood our dark life with golden day,
  Convince, subdue, enthrall;
Then to a mightier yield thy sway,
  And Love be all in all!

Eliza Scudder

56 *So Far, so Near*

O THOU in all thy might so far,
  In all thy love so near,
Beyond the range of sun and star,
  And yet beside us here!

What heart can comprehend thy name,
  Or, searching, find thee out?
Who art, within, a quickening flame,
  A presence round about.

Yet, though I know thee but in part,
  I ask not, Lord, for more:
Enough for me to know thou art.
  To love thee and adore.

Oh, sweeter than aught else besides,
  The tender mystery
That like a veil of shadow hides
  The Light I may not see!

And dearer than all things I know
  Is child-like faith to me,
That makes the darkest way I go
  An open path to thee!

F. L. Hosmer

26

57

Divine Help

O name all other names above,
  What art thou not to me,
Now I have learned to trust thy love
  And cast my care on thee!

What is our being but a cry,
  A restless longing still,
Which thou alone canst satisfy,
  Alone thy fulness fill?

Thrice blessed be the holy souls
  That lead the way to thee,
That burn upon the martyr rolls
  And lists of prophecy!

And sweet it is to tread the ground
  O'er which their faith hath trod;
But sweeter far, when thou art found,
  The soul's own sense of God.

The thought of thee all sorrow calms:
  Our anxious burdens fall;
His crosses turn to triumph-palms
  Who finds in God his all.
                              F. L. Hosmer

58

A Song of Faith

We pray no more, made lowly wise,
  For miracle and sign:
Anoint our eyes to see within
  The common the divine.

We turn, from seeking thee afar
  And in unwonted ways,
To build from out our daily lives
  The temples of thy praise.

And if thy casual comings, Lord,
  To hearts of old were dear,
What joy shall dwell within the faith
  That feels thee ever near!

And nobler yet shall duty grow,
  And more shall worship be,
When thou art found in all our life,
  And all our life in thee.
                              F. L. Hosmer

59

The House our Fathers built to God

We love the venerable house
  Our fathers built to God;
In heaven are kept their grateful vows,
  Their dust endears the sod.

Here, holy thoughts a light have shed
  From many a radiant face,
And prayers of tender hope have spread
  A perfume through the place.

And anxious hearts have pondered here
  The mystery of life,
And prayed the Eternal Spirit clear
  Their doubts and aid their strife.

From humble tenements around
  Came up the pensive train,
And in the church a blessing found,
  Which filled their homes again.

They live with God, their homes are
      dust;
  But here their children pray,
And, in this fleeting lifetime, trust
  To find the narrow way.
                              Ralph Waldo Emerson

27

BALERMA C. M.

60   *On the Field*

OH, blest is he to whom is given
  The instinct that can tell
That God is on the field, when he
  Is most invisible.

And blest is he who can divine
  Where real right doth lie,
And dares to take the side that seems
  Wrong to man's blindfold eye.

Oh, learn to scorn the praise of men!
  Oh, learn to lose — with God!
For Jesus won the world through shame,
  And beckons thee his road.

And right is right, since God is God;
  And right the day must win:
To doubt would be disloyalty,
  To falter would be sin.

F. W. Faber

61   *Breathing after Holiness*

OH, that the Lord would guide my ways
  To keep his statutes still!
Oh, that my God would grant me grace
  To know and do his will!

Oh, send thy Spirit down, to write
  Thy law upon my heart!
Nor let my tongue indulge deceit,
  Nor act the liar's part.

From vanity turn off mine eyes;
  Let no corrupt design,
Nor covetous desires, arise
  Within this soul of mine.

Order my footsteps by thy word,
  And make my heart sincere;
Let sin have no dominion, Lord,
  But keep my conscience clear.

Watts

62 *Speak Gently*

SPEAK gently,— it is better far
  To rule by love than fear;
Speak gently,— let no harsh word mar
  The good we may do here.

Speak gently to the young, for they
  Will have enough to bear:
Pass through this life as best they may,
  'Tis full of anxious care.

Speak gently to the aged one,
  Grieve not the careworn heart.
The sands of life are nearly run,—
  Let them in peace depart.

Speak gently to the erring ones:
  They must have toiled in vain.
Perchance, unkindness made them so;
  Oh, win them back again!

Speak gently,—'tis a little thing
  Dropped in the heart's deep well:
The good, the joy that it may bring,
  Eternity shall tell.

Hanaford

63 *The Universal Prayer*

FATHER of all! in every age,
  In every clime adored,
By saint, by savage, or by sage,
  Jehovah, Jove, or Lord!

Thou great First Cause, least understood,
  Who all my sense confined
To know but this,— that thou art good
  And that myself am blind;

What conscience dictates to be done
  Or warns me not to do,
This teach me more than hell to shun,
  That more than heaven pursue.

If I am right, thy grace impart
  Still in the right to stay;
If I am wrong, Oh, teach my heart
  To find that better way!

Teach me to feel another's woe,
  To hide the fault I see.
The mercy I to others show,
  That mercy show to me.

This day be bread and peace my lot;
  All else beneath the sun
Thou knowest if best bestowed or not,—
  And let thy will be done!

To thee whose temple is all space,
  Whose altar earth, sea, skies,
One chorus let all beings raise,
  All nature's incense rise!

A. Pope

64 *The Book of Nature*

THERE is a book who runs may read,
  Which heavenly truth imparts,
And all the lore its scholars need
  Pure eyes and [earnest] hearts.

The works of God, above, below,
  Within us and around,
Are pages in that book, to show
  How God himself is found.

The glorious sky, embracing all,
  Is like the Maker's love,
Wherewith encompassed, great and small
  In peace and order move.

Thou who hast given us eyes to see
  And love this sight so fair,
Give us a heart to find out thee,
  And read thee everywhere!

Keble

BRATTLE STREET C. M. DOUBLE

65 *The Stream of Faith*

FROM heart to heart, from creed to creed,
  The hidden river runs:
It quickens all the ages down,
  It binds the sires to sons,—
The stream of Faith, whose source is God,
  Whose sound the sound of prayer,
Whose meadows are the holy lives
  Upspringing everywhere.

And still it moves, a broadening flood,
  And fresher, fuller grows,
A sense as if the sea were near
  Toward which the river flows.
O Thou who art the secret Source
  That rises in each soul,
Thou art the Ocean, too,— thy charm
  That ever-deepening roll!

W. C. Gannett

66 *Listening*

I HEAR it often in the dark,
  I hear it in the light,—
Where is the voice that comes to me
  With such a quiet might?
It seems but echo to my thought,
  And yet beyond the stars!
It seems a heart-beat in a hush,
  And yet the planet jars!

Oh, may it be that far within
  My inmost soul there lies
A *spirit-sky*, that opens with
  Those voices of surprise?
Thy heaven is mine,— my very soul!
  Thy words are sweet and strong:
They fill my inward silences
  With music and with song.

They send me challenges to right,
And loud rebuke my ill;
They ring my bells of victory;
They breathe my " Peace, be still! "
They ever seem to say: " My child,
Why seek me so all day?
Now journey inward to thyself,
And listen by the way! "

W. C. Gannett

67   A Song of Trust

O LOVE divine, of all that is
The sweetest still and best,
Fain would I come and rest to-night
Upon thy tender breast.
I pray thee, turn me not away;
For, sinful though I be,
Thou knowest everything I need,
And all my need of thee.

And yet the spirit in my heart
Says, Wherefore should I pray [love,
That thou shouldst seek me with thy
Since thou dost seek alway?
And dost not even wait until
I urge my steps to thee,
But in the darkness of my life
Art coming still to me.

But thou wilt hear the thought I mean
And not the words I say;
Wilt hear the thanks among the words
That only seem to pray.
Still, still thy love will beckon me,
And still thy strength will come
In many ways to bear me up
And bring me to my home.

John W. Chadwick

68   Clouds

A LOWERING sky with heavy clouds
That darken all the day!
'Tis often thus in human life
We walk our clouded way.
But still I know the sun shines on,
Though mist the earth enshrouds:
The sun himself the vapors lifts,
Or there would be no clouds.

It is the sun's glad rays that cast
The shadows wide and deep.
Thus, though I stumble in the dark,
Faith in the light I'll keep.
For he that lifts from marshy lands
These clouds that trail the sky,
Will scatter, melt in rain, or change
To beauty by and by.

M. J. S.

69   The Hymn of Summer

How GLAD the tone when summer's sun
Wreathes the gay world with flowers,
And trees bend down with golden fruit,
And birds are in their bowers.
The morn sends silent music down
Upon each earthly thing;
And always since creation's dawn
The stars together sing.

Shall man remain in silence, then,
While all beneath the skies
The chorus join? No: let us sing;
And, while our voices rise,
Oh, let our lives, great God! breathe forth
A constant melody,
And every action be a tone
In that sweet hymn to thee!

J. Richardson

31

DEDHAM C. M.

70   *Pure Worship*

THE offerings to thy throne which rise,
Of mingled praise and prayer,
Are but a worthless sacrifice,
Unless the heart is there.

Upon thine all-discerning ear
Let no vain words intrude,
No tribute but the vow sincere,—
The tribute of the good.

My offerings will indeed be blest,
If sanctified by thee,
If thy pure spirit touch my breast
With its own purity.

Oh, may that spirit warm my heart
To piety and love,
And to life's lowly vale impart
Some rays from heaven above!

Bowring

71   *The City of God*

CITY of God, how broad and far
Outspread thy walls sublime!
The true thy chartered freemen are
Of every age and clime.

One holy Church, one army strong,
One steadfast high intent,
One working band, one harvest-song,
One King Omnipotent

How purely hath thy speech come down
From man's primeval youth!
How grandly hath thy empire grown
Of Freedom, Love, and Truth!

In vain the surge's angry shock,
In vain the drifting sands,
Unharmed, upon the Eternal Rock.
The Eternal City stands.

S. Johnson

72 *Hymn of Spring*

WHEN warmer suns and bluer skies
Proclaim the opening year,
What happy sounds of life arise,
What lovely scenes appear!

Earth with her thousand voices sings
Her song of gladsome praise,
And every blade of grass that springs
God's loving law obeys.

The early flowers bloom bright and fair,
Fair shines the morning sky,
The birds make music in the air,
The brook goes singing by.

Like this spring morning sweet and clear,
That greets our gladdened eyes,
The spring of heaven's eternal year
Shall bring new earth and skies.

Anon

73 *Effort*

Scorn not the slightest word or deed,
Nor deem it void of power:
There's fruit in each wind-wafted seed
That waits its natal hour.

A whispered word may touch the heart,
And call it back to life;
A look of love bid sin depart,
And still unholy strife.

No act falls fruitless; none can tell
How vast its power may be,
Nor what results infolded dwell
Within it silently.

Work on, despair not; bring thy mite,
Nor care how small it be:
God is with all that serve the right,
The holy, true, and free.

Anon

74 *The Divine Will*

I WORSHIP thee, sweet Will of God,
And all thy ways adore;
And, every day I live, I long
To love thee more and more.

He always wins who sides with God:
To him no chance is lost:
God's will is sweetest to him when
It triumphs at his cost.

Ill that God blesses is our good,
And unblest good is ill; [wrong,
And all is right that seems most
If it be his dear will!

I have no cares, O blessed Will,
For all my cares are thine.
I live in triumph, Lord; for thou
Hast made thy triumphs mine.

Frederic W. Faber

75 *God's Anvil*

I BREATHE the fiery furnace breath;
I feel God's hammer-blows;
I faint as in the grip of death,
As round his hard laws close.

Let me be patient; for 'tis love
Enkindles all the flame.
The blows his faithful kindness prove,
And echo his dear name.

His tender hand, with iron grasp,
Me on the anvil holds; [clasp
His breath the flames that round me
With fiercely-burning folds.

By fiery forge and hammer blow
The ore of life and thought
Are shaped, until their uses show
That skill divine hath wrought.

M. J. S

33

DUNDEE C. M.

76 *The Church Universal*

ONE holy Church of God appears
　Through every age and race,
Unwasted by the lapse of years,
　Unchanged by changing place.

From oldest time, on farthest shores,
　Beneath the pine or palm,
One Unseen Presence she adores,
　With silence or with psalm.

Her priests are all God's faithful sons,
　To serve the world raised up;
The pure in heart her baptized ones;
　Love, her communion-cup.

The truth is her prophetic gift,
　The soul her sacred page;
And feet on mercy's errands swift
　Do make her pilgrimage.

O living Church! thine errand speed,
　Fulfil thy task sublime;
With bread of life earth's hunger feed,—
　Redeem the evil time!

S. Longfellow

77 *All as God wills*

ALL as God wills! who wisely heeds
　To give or to withhold,
And knoweth more of all my needs
　Than all my prayers have told.

Enough, that blessings undeserved
　Have marked my erring track;
That, wheresoe'er my feet have swerved,
　Thy chastening turned me back;

That more and more a providence
　Of love is understood,
Making the springs of time and sense
　Bright with eternal good;

That death seems but a covered way
　Which opens into light,
Wherein no blinded child can stray
　Beyond the Father's sight.

No longer forward or behind
　I look, in hope or fear,
But grateful take the good I find,
　God's blessing now and here.

Whittier

34

78 *Yet Speaketh*

IMMORTAL by their deed and word,
Like light around them shed,
Still speak the prophets of the Lord,
Still live the sainted dead.

The voice of old by Jordan's flood
Yet floats upon the air:
We hear it in beatitude,
In parable and prayer.

And still the beauty of that life
Shines star-like on our way,
And breathes its calm amid the strife
And burden of to-day.

Earnest of life forevermore,
That life of duty here,—
The trust that in the darkest hour
Looked forth and knew no fear.

Spirit of Jesus, still speed on!
Speed on thy conquering way,
Till every heart the Father own,
And all his will obey.
F. L. Hosmer

79 *The Indwelling God*

OH, not in far-off realms of space,
The spirit hath its throne:
In every heart, it findeth place,
And waiteth to be known.

Thought answereth alone to thought,
And soul with soul hath kin:
The outward God he findeth not
Who finds not God within.

And if the vision come to thee,
Revealed by inward sign,
Earth will be full of Deity,
And with his glory shine.

Thou shalt not wait for company,
Nor pitch thy tent alone:
The indwelling God will go with thee,
And show thee of his own.

O gift of gifts, O grace of grace!
That God should condescend
To make thy heart his dwelling-place,
And be thy daily friend!
F. L. Hosmer

80 *Prayer*

FATHER, we would not dare to change
Thy purpose, if we might;
For how shall man presume to teach
The everlasting Right?

No word of ours can make thee wise
Or better than thou art;
And yet we lift our souls to thee
For what thou canst impart.

Our prayer is but a flower that lifts
Its petals to the sun;
That in the light it may unfold
Its leaflets one by one.

We only ask thyself; that we,
Unfolding hour by hour
The beauty of good deeds, may drink
Thy life in like the flower.
M. J. S.

35

81 *Auld Lang Syne*

SHOULD auld acquaintance be forgot,
  And never brought to mind?
Should auld acquaintance be forgot,
  And days of auld lang syne?
For auld lang syne we meet to-night,
  For auld lang syne,
To sing the songs our fathers sang
  In days of auld lang syne.

We've passed through many varied
      scenes,
  Since youth's unclouded day;
And friends and hopes and happy
      dreams
  Time's hand hath swept away;
And voices that once joined with ours,
  In days of auld lang syne,
Are silent now, and blend no more
  In songs of auld lang syne.

But when we cross the sea of life,
  And reach the heavenly shore,
We'll sing the songs our fathers sing,
  Transcending those of yore:

We'll meet to sing diviner strains
  Than those of auld lang syne,—
Immortal songs of praise, unknown
  In days of auld lang syne.

  Anon

82 *Song of the Silent Ones*

IT singeth low in every heart,
  We hear it each and all,—
A song of those who answer not,
  However we may call.
They throng the silence of the breast;
  We see them as of yore,—
The kind, the true, the brave, the sweet,
  Who walk with us no more.

'Tis hard to take the burden up,
  When these have laid it down:
They brightened all the joy of life,
  They softened every frown.
But, oh! 'tis good to think of them
  When we are troubled sore;
Thanks be to God that such have been,
  Although they are no more!

36

More homelike seems the vast unknown,
  Since they have entered there;
To follow them were not so hard,
  Wherever they may fare.
They cannot be where God is not,
  On any sea or shore.
Whate'er betides, thy love abides,
  Our God, for evermore!
                              John W. Chadwick

83   *Summer Days*

THE summer days are come again;
  Once more, the glad earth yields
Her golden wealth of ripening grain,
  And breath of clover-fields;
And deepening shade of summer woods,
  And glow of summer air,
And winging thoughts, and happy words
  Of love and joy and prayer.

The summer days are come again,
  The birds are on the wing;
God's praises, in their loving strain,
  Unconsciously they sing.
We *know* who giveth all the good
  That doth our cup o'erbrim:
For summer joy in field and wood,
  We lift our song to Him.
                              S. Longfellow

84   *Serving Man*

THE cattle on a thousand hills
  With all their flocks are thine;
The corn that waves in every vale,
  The grape and all its wine.
We cannot minister to Thee
  Who everything dost own:
Our duty we can only pay
  By serving man alone.

To teach the world's dark ignorance,
  To lift up those that fall,
To cheer the sad, and stoop to hear
  The needy when they call,—
This is an offering worthy God,
  A sacrifice divine.
With hearts and hands made holy thus,
  We may approach his shrine.
                              M. J. E.

85   *Heroic Memories*

WE'LL sing our loving trust in God,
  However dark the day;
For sure 'tis he who leadeth us
  Along our changeful way.
There cometh sun, there cometh cloud;
  But, whate'er may befall,
We still will follow after him
  Who leads us through them all.

We'll cheer our hearts, as on we go,
  With thoughts of those of old,
Who through their furnace-trials came
  Refined like precious gold.
Like Jesus, they, too, stood for truth,
  Though heretic with men;
Like him, they triumphed, though they
      died,
  And still they live again.

Not only in the far-off lands
  And far-off times they wrought:
The modern world has heroes too
  To lift its heart and thought.
These are the ones who dare to think;
  And, spite of hostile wrath,
They, for the progress of mankind,
  Hew out a grander path.
                              M. J. S.

PETERBOROUGH   C. M.

86   *Nature's Worship*

THE harp at Nature's advent strung
  Has never ceased to play;
The song the stars of morning sung
  Has never died away.

The green earth sends her incense up
  From many a mountain shrine;
From folded leaf and dewy cup,
  She pours her sacred wine.

The blue sky is the temple's arch;
  Its transept, earth and air;
The music of its starry march,
  The chorus of a prayer.

So Nature keeps the reverent frame
  With which her years began,
And all her signs and voices shame
  The prayerless heart of man.

J. G. Whittier

87   *Who is thy Neighbor*

WHO is thy neighbor? He whom thou
  Hast power to aid or bless;
Whose aching heart or burning brow
  Thy soothing hand may press.

Thy neighbor? 'Tis the fainting poor,
  Whose eye with want is dim:
Oh, enter thou his humble door,
  With aid and peace for him!

Thy neighbor? He who drinks the cup
  When sorrow drowns the brim.
With words of high, sustaining hope,
  Go thou and comfort him.

Thy neighbor? Pass no mourner by.
  Perhaps thou canst redeem
A breaking heart from misery:
  Go share thy lot with him.

Peabody

88 *Walk in the Light*

WALK in the light! so shalt thou know
That fellowship of love
His Spirit only can bestow,
Who reigns in light above.

Walk in the light! and thou shalt find
Thy heart made truly his,
Who dwells in cloudless light enshrined,
In whom no darkness is.

Walk in the light! and thou shalt own
Thy darkness passed away;
Because that light hath on thee shone,
In which is perfect day.

Walk in the light! and thine shall be
A path, though thorny, bright;
For God, by grace, shall dwell in thee,
And God himself is light.

Bernard Barton

89 *A New Year*

OUR Father, through the coming year
We know not what shall be;
But we would leave, without a fear,
Its ordering all to thee.

It may be we shall toil in vain
For what the world holds fair;
And all its good we thought to gain
Deceive, and prove but care.

It may be it shall bring us days
And nights of lingering pain,
And bid us take our farewell gaze
Of these loved haunts of men.

But calmly, Lord, on thee we rest:
No fears our trust shall move;
Thou knowest what for each is best;
And thou art perfect love.

Gaskell

90 *Kindly Judgment*

THINK gently of the erring one:
Oh, let us not forget,
However darkly stained by sin,
He is our brother yet!

Heir of the same inheritance,
Child of the self-same God,
He hath but fallen in the path
We have in weakness trod.

Speak gently to the erring ones:
We may yet lead them back,
With holy words and tones of love,
From misery's thorny track.

Forget not, brother, thou hast sinned,
And sinful yet may'st be:
Deal gently with the erring heart,
As God hath dealt with thee.

Miss Fletcher

91 *I will sing of thy Power and thy Mercy*

OUR Father, God! thy gracious power
On every hand we see:
Oh, may the blessings of each hour
Lead all our thoughts to thee!

If, on the wings of morn, we speed
To earth's remotest bound,
Thy hand will there our footsteps lead,
Thy love our path surround.

Thy power is in the ocean deeps,
And reaches to the skies;
Thine eye of mercy never sleeps,
Thy goodness never dies.

In all the varying scenes of time,
On thee our hopes depend,—
Through every age, in every clime,
Our Father and our friend!

James Thomson

NAOMI C. M.

92 *A Thankful Heart*

FATHER, whate'er of earthly bliss
Thy sovereign hand denies,
Accepted at thy throne of grace,
Let this petition rise:

Give me a calm, a thankful heart,
From every murmur free;
The blessings of thy grace impart,
And make me live to thee.

Let the sweet thought that thou art mine
My life and death attend;
Thy presence through my journey shine,
And crown my journey's end.

Anne Steele

93 *Jesus of Nazareth*

THE loving Friend to all who bowed
Beneath life's weary load,
From lips baptized in humble prayer
His consolations flowed.

The faithful Witness to the Truth,
His just rebuke was hurled
Out from a heart that burned to break
The fetters of the world.

No hollow rite, no lifeless creed,
His piercing glance could bear;
But longing hearts which sought him found
That God and heaven were there.

S. Longfellow

94 *Leading the Way*

ANOTHER hand is beckoning us,
Another call is given;
And glows once more with angel steps
The path that leads to heaven.

Oh, half we deemed she needed not
The changing of her sphere,
To give to heaven a shining one,
Who walked an angel here!

Unto our Father's will alone
One thought hath reconciled,—
That he whose love exceedeth ours
Hath taken home his child.

Fold her, O Father, in thine arms,
And let her henceforth be
A messenger of love between
Our human hearts and thee.

40

Still, let her mild rebuking stand
　Between us and the wrong,
And her dear memory serve to make
　Our faith in goodness strong.
Whittier

95 *Death of the Righteous*

BEHOLD the western evening light!
　It melts in deepening gloom :
So calm the righteous sink away,
　Descending to the tomb.

The winds breathe low ; the yellow leaf
　Scarce whispers from the tree :
So gently flows the parting breath,
　When good men cease to be.

How beautiful, on all the hills,
　The crimson light is shed !
'Tis like the peace the dying gives
　To mourners round his bed.

How mildly, on the wandering cloud,
　The sunset beam is cast !
So sweet the memory left behind,
　When loved ones breathe their last.

And, lo ! above the dews of night
　The vesper star appears :
So faith lights up the mourner's heart
　Whose eyes are dim with tears.
William B. O. Peabody

96 *" Blessed are they that mourn "*

FROM lips divine, like healing balm
　To hearts oppressed and torn,
The heavenly consolation fell,
　" Blessed are they that mourn."

Unto the hopes by sorrow crushed,
　A noble faith succeeds ;
And life, by trials furrowed, bears
　The fruit of loving deeds.

How rich, how sweet, how full of
　strength
　Our human spirits are,
Baptized into the sanctities
　Of suffering and of prayer !

Yes, heavenly wisdom, love divine,
　Breathed through the lips which said,
" Oh, blessed are the hearts that mourn :
　They shall be comforted."
William H. Burleigh

97 *All Truth leads to God*

FATHER, by whatsoever light
　Our path of life we see,
It matters not, so at the last
　It leadeth us to thee.

We thank thee for the star that rose
　O'er old Judea bright ;
And that its deathless ray still shines,
　To fill our souls with light.

We thank thee, too, that other stars
　O'er other lands have shone,
To guide the stumbling feet of those
　Who toward thee struggle on.

Thou, many names of saving power,
　Hast given unto men ;
And each new truth that lifts the world
　Is God come down again.
M. J. S.

98 *Another Year*

ANOTHER year of setting suns,
  Of stars by night revealed,
Of springing grass, of tender buds
  By winter's snow concealed.

Another year of summer's glow,
  Of autumn's gold and brown,
Of waving fields, and ruddy fruit
  The branches weighing down.

Another year of happy work
  That better is than play ;
Of simple cares, and love that grows
  More sweet from day to day.

Another year of baby mirth,
  And childhood's blessed ways;
Of thinker's thought, and prophet's
And poet's tender lays.   [dream,

Another year at Beauty's feast,
  At every moment spread ;
Of silent hours, when grow distinct
  The voices of the dead.

Another year to follow hard
  Where better souls have trod ;
Another year of life's delight;
  Another year of God !
                    J. W. Chadwick

99 *Thy Kingdom come*

O GOD, the darkness roll away,
  Which clouds the human soul;
And let the bright, the perfect day
  Speed onward to its goal.

Let every hateful passion die,
  Which makes of brethren foes;
And war no longer raise its cry
  To mar the world's repose.

Let faith and hope and charity
  Go forth through all the earth;
And man, in heavenly bearing, be
  True to his heavenly birth.

Yea, let thy glorious kingdom come,
  Of holiness and love;
And make this world a portal meet
  For thy bright courts above.
                    William Gaskell

42

MARLOW C. M.

100 *Spring*

THE softened mould is brown and warm,
  The early blossoms break,
And loosened streams along their banks
  A mossy verdure make.

A dewy light broods o'er the earth,
  A sweetness new and rare,
And tumults of brook, bird, and breeze
  With music wake the air.

Awake, O heart! awake and learn
  The secret of the spring!
From winter-sleep it comes like light,
  Or as a bird on wing.

And if I shall be winter-locked,
  As sometime I may be;
If bitter storms and freezing snows
  Come whirling down on me,—

Let me lie patient, like the earth,
  And say, "This shall be rest";
And then, O Lord! at thy dear call
  Arise renewed and blest.
                              J. V. Blake

101 *Assured*

I LONG for household voices gone,
  For vanished smiles, I long;
But God hath led my dear ones on,
  And he can do no wrong.

I know not what the future hath
  Of marvel and surprise,
Assured alone that life and death
  His mercy underlies.

And, if my heart and flesh are weak
  To bear an untried pain,
The bruised reed he will not break,
  But strengthen and sustain.

I know not where his islands lift
  Their fronded palms in air;
I only know I cannot drift
  Beyond his love and care.

And so beside the Silent Sea
  I wait the muffled oar:
No harm from him can come to me
  On ocean or on shore.
                            J. G. Whittier

MANOAH C. M.

102 *Evolution*

THE one life thrilled the star-dust
through,
In nebulous masses whirled,
Until, globed like a drop of dew,
Shone out a new-made world.

The one life on the ocean shore,
Through primal ooze and slime,
Crept slowly on from less to more
Along the ways of time.

The one life in the jungles old,
From lowly, creeping things,
Did ever some new form unfold,—
Swift feet or soaring wings.

The one life all the ages through
Pursued its wondrous plan,
Till, as the tree of promise grew,
It blossomed into man.

The one life reacheth onward still:
As yet, no eye may see

The far-off fact man's dream fulfil,—
The glory yet to be.

M. J. S.

103 *Hope*

STANDING upon the mountain top,
We catch the kindling ray
That reddens in the east, and tells
The coming of the day.

The valleys all in shadow lie,
And dark is every plain :
It seems as if the world's long night
Would never cease its reign.

But when the eastern hill-tops glow,
We know the night is past ;
And, though the valleys still are dark,
The day must come at last.

Thus Hope her cheering lesson reads
In every dawn of day :
How slow soe'er the shadows lift,
The night must pass away.

M. J. S.

44

WOODSTOCK C. M.

104
The Manifold Grace of God

Thou Grace divine, encircling all,
A shoreless, soundless sea,
Wherein at last our souls must fall,—
O love of God most free!

When over dizzy heights we go,
One soft hand blinds our eyes,
The other leads us safe and slow,—
O love of God most wise!

And though we turn us from thy face,
And wander wide and long,
Thou hold'st us still in thine embrace,—
O love of God most strong!

The saddened heart, the restless soul,
The toil-worn frame and mind,
Alike confess thy sweet control,—
O love of God most kind!

And, filled and quickened by thy breath,
Our souls are strong and free

To rise o'er sin and fear and death,
O love of God, to thee!

Eliza Scudder

105
Aspiration

The dove, let loose in eastern skies,
Returning fondly home,
Ne'er stoops to earth her wing, nor flies
Where idle warblers roam.

But high she shoots through air and light,
Above all low delay,
Where nothing earthly bounds her flight,
Nor shadow dims her way.

So grant me, Lord, from every snare
Of sinful passion free,
Aloft, through faith's serener air,
To urge my course to thee;

No sin to cloud, no lure to stay
My soul, as home she springs,—
Thy sunshine on her joyful way,
Thy freedom on her wings.

T. Moore

45

BARBY C.M.

106 *Man frail, and God eternal*

O God, our help in ages past,
　Our hope for years to come,
Our shelter from the stormy blast,
　And our eternal home,—

Before the hills in order stood,
　Or earth received her frame,
From everlasting thou art God,
　To endless years the same.

A thousand ages, in thy sight,
　Are like an evening gone;
Short as the watch that ends the night,
　Before the rising sun.

Time, like an ever-rolling stream
　Bears all its sons away;
They fly, forgotten, as a dream
　Dies at the opening day.

O God, our help in ages past,
　Our hope for years to come,

Be thou our guard while troubles last,
　And our eternal home!

Isaac Watts

107 *The Ways of Wisdom*

Wisdom has treasures greater far
　Than east or west unfold,
And her rewards more precious are
　Than is the gain of gold.

In her right hand she holds to view
　A length of happy years,
And in her left the prize of fame
　And honor bright appears.

She guides the young with innocence
　In pleasure's path to tread,
A crown of glory she bestows
　Upon the hoary head.

According as her labors rise,
　So her rewards increase:
Her ways are ways of pleasantness,
　And all her paths are peace.

Scotch Paraphrases

46

AZMON   C. M.

108 *Laying a Corner-stone of a Church*

THE heavens cannot contain thee, Lord;
    And shall we think to raise
Fit dwelling for thy living word
    Or worthy of thy praise?

Shall walls of wood or stone, reared
    high,
    Look noble in thy sight?
Or lofty spire that cleaves the sky
    Touch heaven with delight?

Nay, these are senseless! thou wouldst
    have
    A temple built of men,
Compact with deeds that seek to save
    And lift to God again.

The utmost truth of God and man
    Shall be our corner-stone;
And rising walls unfold a plan
    That Love may call her own.

Thus may thy holy church arise,
    Until the structure fair
Shall fill the earth and touch the skies,
    And heaven be everywhere.

M. J. S.

109   *Consecration*

O GOD, whose law is in the sky,
    Whose light is on the sea,
Who livest in the human heart,
    We give ourselves to thee.

In fearless, world-wide search for truth,
    Whatever form it wear,
Or crown or cross or fame or blame,
    We thine ourselves declare.

In love that binds mankind in one,
    That serves all those in need,
Whose law is helpful sympathy,—
    In this we're thine indeed.

In labor, whose far-distant end
    Is bringing to accord
The real fact with highest hope,
    We follow thee, O Lord!

To truth, to love, to duty, then,
    Wherever we may be,
We give ourselves! and, doing this,
    We give ourselves to thee.

M. J. S.

47

LABAN S. M.

110 *In Calm and Storm*

IF, on a quiet sea,
Toward heaven we calmly sail,
With grateful hearts, O God! to thee
We owe the favoring gale.

But should the surges rise,
And rest delay to come,
Blest be the sorrow, kind the storm,
Which drives us nearer home!

Soon shall our doubts and fears
All yield to thy control;
Thy tender mercies shall illume
The midnight of the soul.

Teach us in every state
To make thy will our own,
And, when the joys of sense depart,
To live by faith alone.

Anon

111 *The Sower*

Sow IN the morn thy seed,
At eve hold not thy hand;
To doubt and fear, give thou no heed,
Broadcast it o'er the land!

Beside all waters sow,
The highway furrows stock,
Drop it where thorns and thistles grow,
Scatter it on the rock!

And duly shall appear,
In verdure, beauty, strength,
The tender blade, the stalk, the ear,
And the full corn at length.

James Montgomery

112 *Heaven Everywhere*

OUR heaven is everywhere,
If we but love the Lord,
Unswerving tread the narrow way,
And ever shun the broad.

'Tis where the trusting heart
Bows meekly to its grief,
Still looking up with earnest faith
For comfort and relief.

Wherever truth abides,
Sweet peace is ever there :
If we but love and serve the Lord,
Our heaven is everywhere.

48

113 *The Lord's Prayer*

OUR heavenly Father, hear
The prayer we offer now!
Thy name be hallowed far and near,
To thee, all nations bow.

Thy kingdom come; thy will
On earth be done in love,
As saints and seraphim fulfil
Thy perfect law above.

Our daily bread supply,
While by thy word we live;
The guilt of our iniquity
Forgive as we forgive.

From dark temptation's power
Our feeble hearts defend;
Deliver in the evil hour,
And guide us to the end.

Thine, then, for ever be
Glory and power divine!
The sceptre, throne, and majesty
Of heaven and earth are thine.

James Montgomery

114 *The Right is the Beautiful*

TEACH me, my God and King,
Thy will in all to see,
And what I do in anything
To do it as for thee!

To scorn the senses' sway,
While still to thee I tend.
In all I do be thou the way,
In all be thou the end.

All may of thee partake ·
Nothing so small can be
But draws, when acted for thy sake,
Greatness and worth from thee.

A servant with this clause
Makes drudgery divine :
Who sweeps a room as for thy laws
Makes that and th' action fine.

This is the famous stone
That turneth all to gold;
For that which God doth touch and own
Cannot for less be told.

George Herbert

49

ST. THOMAS S. M.

115 *The Lord shall lead me*

Thy way, not mine, O Lord!
However dark it be:
Lead me aright by thine own hand,
Choose out the path for me.

Smooth let it be or rough,
It will be still the best;
Winding or straight, it matters not,
It leads me to thy rest.

I dare not choose my lot;
I would not if I might:
Choose thou the way for me, my God,
So shall I walk aright.

Not mine, not mine the choice
In things or great or small:
Be thou my light, my guide, my strength,
My wisdom, and my all.

Bonar

116 *"Thy Kingdom Come"*

Come, kingdom of our God,
Sweet reign of light and love,
Shed peace and hope and joy abroad,
And wisdom from above.

Over our spirits first
Extend thy healing reign:
There raise and quench the sacred thirst
That never pains again.

Come, kingdom of our God,
And make the broad earth thine;
Stretch o'er her lands and isles the rod
That flowers with grace divine.

Soon may all tribes be blest
With fruit from life's glad tree,
And in its shade like brothers rest,
Sons of one family.

Johns

117 *"It is nigh Thee, in thy Heart"*

Say not the law divine
Is hidden far from thee:
That heavenly law within may shine,
And there its brightness be.

Soar not, my soul, on high,
To bring it down to earth:
No star within the vaulted sky
Is of such priceless worth.

50

Thou need'st nòt launch thy bark
Upon a shoreless sea,
Breasting its waves to find the ark,
To bring this dove to thee.

Cease, then, my soul, to roam;
Thy wanderings all are vain:
That holy word is found at home,
Within thy heart its reign.

Barton

118 *Brotherhood*

HUSH the loud cannon's roar,
The frantic warrior's call! [gore?
Why should the earth be drenched with
Are we not brothers all?

Want, from the wretch depart!
Chains, from the captive fall!
Sweet Mercy, melt the oppressor's heart
Sufferers are brothers all.

Churches and sects, strike down
Each mean partition-wall!
Let Love each harsher feeling drown;
For men are brothers all.

Let Love and Truth alone
Hold human hearts in thrall,
That Heaven its work at length may own,
And men be brothers all.

Johns

119 *The True Fast*

"Is THIS a fast for me?"
Thus saith the Lord our God:
"A day for man to vex his soul,
And feel affliction's rod?

"No: is not this alone
The sacred fast I choose,—
Oppression's yoke to burst in twain,
The bands of guilt unloose?

"To nakedness and want,
Your food and raiment deal;
To dwell your kindred race among,
And all their sufferings heal?

"Then, like the morning ray,
Shall spring your health and light:
Before you, righteousness shall shine;
Behind, my glory bright."

Drummond

51

BROWNE S. M. DOUBLE

120 *The Pilgrim Fathers*

THE breaking waves dashed high
  On a stern and rock-bound coast;
And the woods against a stormy sky
  Their giant branches tossed;
And the heavy night hung dark
  The hills and waters o'er,—
When a band of exiles moored their
    bark
  On the wild New England shore,

Not as the conqueror comes,
  They, the true-hearted, came;
Not with the roll of stirring drums,
  And the trump that sings of fame:
Not as the flying come,
  In silence and in fear:
They shook the depths of the desert's
    gloom
  With their hymns of lofty cheer.

Amidst the storm they sang:
  And the stars heard, and the sea;
And the sounding aisles of the dim wood
    rang
  With the anthem of the free.
The ocean eagle soared   [foam,
  From his nest by the white wave's
And the rocking pines of the forest
    roared,—
  This was their welcome home!

What sought they thus afar,—
  Bright jewels of the mine,
The wealth of seas, the spoils of war?
  They sought a faith's pure shrine.
Ay, call it holy ground,—
  The soil where first they trod:
They have left unstained what there they
    found,—
  Freedom to worship God.
                          Mrs. Hemans

52

121   *"Happy New Year"*

BACKWARD looking o'er the past,
Forward, too, with eager gaze,
Stand we here to-day, O God!
At the parting of the ways.

Tenderest thoughts our bosoms fill;
Memories all bright and fair
Seem to float on spirit-wings
Downward through the silent air.

Hark! through all their music sweet,
Hear you not a voice of cheer?
'Tis the voice of Hope which sings,
"Happy be the coming year!"

Father, comes that voice from thee!
Swells it with thy meaning vast,—
Good in all thy future stored,
Fairer than in all the past!

             J. W. Chadwick

122   *The Eternal Lights*

SLOWLY, by God's hand unfurled,
Down around the weary world,
Falls the darkness; oh, how still
Is the working of his will!

Mighty Spirit, ever nigh,
Work in me as silently;
Veil the day's distracting sights,
Show me heaven's eternal lights.

Living stars to view be brought
In the boundless realms of thought;
High and infinite desires,
Flaming like those upper fires.

Holy Truth, Eternal Right,
Let them break upon my sight;
Let them shine serene and still,
And with light my being fill!

             Furness

123 *Heredity*

Heir of all the ages, I,—
Heir of all that they have wrought!
All their store of emprise high,
All their wealth of precious thought!

Every golden deed of theirs
Sheds its lustre on my way;
All their labors, all their prayers,
Sanctify this present day.

Heir of all that they have earned
By their passion and their tears;
Heir of all that they have learned
Through the weary, toiling years;

Heir of all the faith sublime
On whose wings they soared to heaven;
Heir of every hope that Time
To earth's fainting sons hath given;

Aspirations pure and high;
Strength to do and to endure;
Heir of all the ages, I,—
Lo, I am no longer poor!

Julia C. R. Dorr

124 *In Common Things*

In each breeze that wanders free,
In each flower that gems the sod,
Living souls may hear and see
Freshly uttered words from God.

Had we but a searching mind,
Seeking good where'er it springs,
We should then true wisdom find
Hidden in familiar things.

God is present and doth shine
Through each scene beneath the sky,
Kindling with a light divine
Every form that meets the eye.

Worlds on worlds in phalanx deep
Need we not to prove him here:
Daisies, fresh from nature's sleep,
Tell of him in lines as clear.

If the mind would Nature see,
Let her cherish Virtue more:
Goodness bears the golden key
That unlocks her temple door.

Mrs. Waterston

125 *The Builders*

ALL are architects of Fate,
Working in these walls of Time:
Some with massive deeds and great,
Some with ornaments of rhyme.

Nothing useless is or low :
Each thing in its place is best ;
And what seems but idle show
Strengthens and supports the rest.

For the structure that we raise,
Time is with materials filled :
Our to-days and yesterdays
Are the blocks with which we build.

Build to-day, then, strong and sure,
With a firm and ample base ;
And ascending and secure
Shall to-morrow find its place.

Longfellow

126 *Education*

LEARNERS are we all at school,
Eager youth and weary age,
Governed by the self-same rule,
Poring o'er the self-same page.

Life the lesson that we learn
As the days and years go by ;
Wondrous are the leaves we turn
On the earth and in the sky.

Oft our sight with tears is blurred
While we strive in vain to tell
What may mean some harder word
Than our wisdom yet can spell.

But we read enough to trust
That our grand hopes are not .ies,
That our hearts are more than dust,
And our homes are in the skies.

M. J. S.

127 *Duty*

THOU, whose name is blazoned forth
On our banner's gleaming fold,
Freedom! all thy sacred worth
Never yet has half been told.

But to-day we sing of one
Older, graver far than thou;
With the seal of time begun
Stamped upon her awful brow.

She is Duty: in her hand
Is a sceptre heaven-brought;
Hers the accent of command,
Hers the dreadful, mystic *Ought*.

But her bondage is so sweet!
And her burdens make us strong:
Wings they seem to weary feet,
Laughter to our lips, and song.

Wheresoever she may lead,
Freshly burdened every day,
Freedom, make us free to speed
In her ever brightening way!

J. W. Chadwick

128   *"Give us our Daily Bread"*

DAY by day, the manna fell:
Oh, to learn this lesson well!
Still by constant mercy fed,
Give me, Lord, my daily bread.

Day by day, the promise reads,—
"Daily strength for daily needs:
Cast foreboding fears away;
Take the manna of to-day."

Lord, my times are in thy hand:
All my sanguine hopes have planned
To thy wisdom I resign,
And would mould my will to thine.

Thou my daily task shalt give;
Day by day to thee I live:
So shall added years fulfil
Not my own, my Father's will.

Josiah Conder

CHATHAM 7s

I29   *Struggle*

THERE's a strife we all must wage,
From life's entrance to its close;
Blest the bold who dare engage!
Woe for him who seeks repose!

Honored they who firmly stand
While the conflict presses round,
God's own banner in their hand,
In his service faithful found.

What our foes? Each thought impure,
Passions fierce that tear the soul,
Every ill that we can cure,
Every crime we can control,

Every suffering which our hand
Can with soothing care assuage,
Every evil of our land,
Every error of our age.

On, then, to the glorious field!
He who dies his life shall save:
God himself shall be our shield,
He shall bless and crown the brave.

Bulfinch

I30   *Inspiration*

LIFE of Ages, richly poured,
Love of God, unspent and free,
Flowing in the prophet's word
And the people's liberty!

Never was to chosen race
That unstinted tide confined:
Thine is every time and place,
Fountain sweet of heart and mind!

Breathing in the thinker's creed,
Pulsing in the hero's blood,
Nerving simplest thought and deed,
Freshening time with truth and good,

Consecrating art and song,
Holy book and pilgrim track,
Hurling floods of tyrant wrong
From the sacred limits back,—

Life of Ages, richly poured,
Love of God, unspent and free,
Flow still in the prophet's word
And the people's liberty!

S. Johnson

131 *Beauty for Ashes*

Leaf by leaf the roses fall,
Drop by drop the springs run dry,
One by one, beyond recall,
Summer beauties fade and die.
But the roses bloom again,
And the springs will gush anew,
In the pleasant April rain
And the summer sun and dew.

So, in hours of deepest gloom,
When the springs of gladness fail,
And the roses in their bloom
Droop like maidens wan and pale,
We shall find some hope that lies
Like a silent germ apart,
Hidden far from careless eyes
In the garden of the heart;

Some sweet hope, to gladness wed,
That will spring afresh and new
When grief's winter shall have fled,
Giving place to sun and dew;
Some sweet hope that breathes of spring
Through the weary, weary time,
Budding forth its blossoming
In the spirit's silent clime.

Howe

132 *Social Love*

When the truth shall lead us home,
When we to its temple come,
Then we shall its goodness prove,
As the only source of love.
Hither all your music bring;
Strike aloud its cheerful string:
Mortals join, the truth approve,—
Join to hail the Source of Love.

Old and young, your voices raise;
Tune your lips in social praise;
Strike the notes upon the lyre:
All to happiness aspire.
Cease contention, discord, strife;
Lessen all the cares of life:
Virtue ne'er can disapprove
Cordial hearts of social love.

Anon

133 *On the Watch-Tower*

WATCHMAN, tell us of the night,—
What its signs of promise are.
Traveller, o'er yon mountain's height,
See that glory-beaming star!
Watchman, does its beauteous ray
Aught of hope or joy foretell?
Traveller, yes: it brings the day,—
Promised day of Israel.

Watchman, tell us of the night:
Higher yet that star ascends.
Traveller, blessedness and light,
Peace and truth, its course portends.
Watchman, will its beams alone
Gild the spot that gave them birth?
Traveller, ages are its own:
See! it bursts o'er all the earth.

Watchman, tell us of the night;
For the morning seems to dawn.
Traveller, darkness takes its flight,
Doubt and terror are withdrawn.

Watchman, let thy wanderings cease:
Hie thee to thy quiet home.
Traveller, lo! the Prince of Peace,
Lo! the Son of God is come.

Bowring

134 *The Offering*

LORD, what offering shall we bring
At thine altars when we bow?
Hearts, the pure, unsullied spring
Whence the kind affections flow;
Quiet thoughts at peace with all;
Wrongs forgiven into rest;
Sympathy intent to call
Sorrow from the wounded breast;

Willing hands to lead the blind,
Bind the wounded, feed the poor;
Love, embracing all our kind,
Charity, with liberal store.
Teach us, O thou heavenly King!
Thus to show our grateful mind,
Thus the accepted offering bring,—
Love to thee and all mankind.

John Taylor

CHESTER 8s & 7s

135 *Seeking God*

Teach us, Father, how to find thee!
This the cry of all the earth.
Search for God has built all altars;
Here have all religions birth.

Lo how simple is the pathway!
God is never far to find ;
Only be like him in helping,
Serve and lift up all mankind.

Pity sorrow, save the sinning,
Lead the little feet, and see!
Helping like God, ye are godlike:
God himself is found in thee.

M. J. S.

136 *God is Love*

God is love: his mercy brightens
All the path in which we rove;
Bliss he wakes, and woe he lightens:
God is wisdom, God is love.

Chance and change are busy ever;
Man decays and ages move;
But his mercy waneth never:
God is wisdom, God is love.

E'en the hour that darkest seemeth
Will his changeless goodness prove;
From the gloom his brightness stream-
God is wisdom, God is love.   [eth:

He with earthly cares entwineth
Hope and comfort from above;
Everywhere his glory shineth:
God is wisdom, God is love.

Bowring

137 *The Gentle Teacher*

Ever find I joy in reading,
In the ancient holy Book,
Of the gentle Teacher's pleading,
Truth in every word and look.

How, when children came, he blessed
    them,
Suffered no man to reprove,
Took them in his arms, and pressed them
To his heart with words of love;

How to all the sick and tearful
Help was ever gladly shown;
How he sought the poor and fearful,
Called them brothers and his own;

How no contrite soul e'er sought him ,
  And was bidden to depart;
How with gentle words he taught him,
  Took the death from out his heart.

Still I read the ancient story,
  And my joy is ever new,—
How he lived so pure and holy,
  How he loved so firm and true.
     Luise Hensel (tr. by Cath. Winkworth)

138   *Decoration Day*

WE remember thee, O brave ones
  Who for truth and country bled!
And, though with us here no longer,
  Still we cannot think thee dead.

Ye are living, though the grasses
  Green above your graves may be:
Ye are living in the glory
  Of a people that is free;

Ye are living in the comrades
  That your faith and valor knew;
Ye shall live in all the future,
  While to right brave men are true.

For no deed heroic faileth
  Ever from the hearts of men:
Each new year it springeth upward,
  Young with endless life again.
     M. J. S.

139   *The City of God*

GLORIOUS things of thee are spoken,
  Zion, city of our God:
He, whose word cannot be broken,
  Formed thee for his own abode.

On the Rock of Ages founded,
  What can shake thy sure repose?

With salvation's walls surrounded,
  Thou mayst smile at all thy foes.

See! the streams of living waters,
  Springing from eternal love,
Well supply thy sons and daughters,
  And all fear of want remove.

Who can faint while such a river
  Ever flows their thirst to assuage!
Grace which, like the Lord the Giver,
  Never fails from age to age.
     J. Newton

140   *The Conflict of Life*

ONWARD [onward], though the region
  Where thou art be drear and lone:
God hath set a guardian legion
  Very near thee,— press thou on!

By the thorn-road, and none other,
  Is the mount of vision won;
Tread it without shrinking, brother!
  Jesus trod it,— press thou on!

By thy trustful, calm endeavor,
  Guiding, cheering, like the sun,
Earth-bound hearts thou shalt deliver:
  Oh, for their sake, press thou on!

Be this world the wiser, stronger,
  For thy life of pain and peace:
While it needs thee, oh, no longer
  Pray thou for thy quick release.

Pray thou [every day the] rather
  That thou be a faithful son;
By the prayer of Jesus,— "Father,
  Not my will, but thine, be done!"
     Samuel Johnson

SICILY 8s & 7s

141   *Psalm of Life*

TELL me not in mournful numbers
  Life is but an empty dream;
For the soul is dead that slumbers,
  And things are not what they seem.

Life is real, life is earnest,
  And the grave is not its goal:
Dust thou art, to dust returnest,
  Was not spoken of the soul.

Not enjoyment, and not sorrow,
  Is our destined end and way;
But to act, that each to-morrow
  Find us further than to-day.

Trust no Future, howe'er pleasant;
  Let the dead Past bury its dead:
Act, act in the living Present,
  Heart within and God o'erhead.

Let us, then, be up and doing,
  With a heart for any fate!
Still achieving, still pursuing,
  Learn to labor and to wait.

Longfellow

142   *Life's Work*

ALL around us, fair with flowers,
  Fields of sleeping beauty lie;
All around us clarion voices
  Call to duty stern and high.

Thankfully we will rejoice in
  All the beauty God has given;
But beware it does not win us
  From the work ordained of heaven.

Following every voice of mercy
  With a trusting, loving heart,
Let us in life's earnest labor
  Still be sure to do our part.

Now, to-day, and not to-morrow,
  Let us work with all our might,
Lest the wretched faint and perish
  In the coming stormy night.

Now, to-day, and not to-morrow,
  Lest, before to-morrow's sun,
We, too, mournfully departing,
  Shall have left our work undone.

Anon

WILMOT 8 & 7s

143 *One by One*

ONE by one the sands are flowing,
 One by one the moments fall :
Some are coming, some are going ;
 Do not strive to grasp them all.

One by one thy duties wait thee ;
 Let thy whole strength go to each ;
Let no future dreams elate thee ;
 Learn thou first what these can teach.

One by one, bright gifts from heaven,
 Joys are lent thee here below ;
Take them readily when given ;
 Ready, too, to let them go.

One by one thy griefs shall meet thee ;
 Do not fear an arméd band :
One will fade as others greet thee,—
 Shadows passing through the land.

Every hour that fleets so slowly
 Has its task to do or bear ;
Luminous the crown and holy,
 If thou set each gem with care.

A. A. Procter

144 *Work*

WORK ! it is thy highest mission.
 Work ! all blessing centres there.
Work for culture, for the vision
 Of the true and good and fair.

'Tis of knowledge the condition,
 Opening still new fields beyond ;
'Tis of thought the full fruition ;
 'Tis of love the perfect bond.

Work ! by labor comes th' unsealing
 Of the thoughts that in thee burn ;
Comes in action the revealing
 Of the truths thou hast to learn.

Work in helping, loving union
 With thy brethren of mankind :
With the foremost hold communion,
 Succor those who toil behind.

For true work can never perish,
 And thy followers in the way
For thy works thy name shall cherish :
 Work while it is called to-day !

F. M. White

SICILY 8s & 7s

145 *Step by Step*

Nor so fearful, doubting pilgrim,
  Though the darkness round thee
      close,
Though the future glooms foreboding,
  Threatening all thy soul's repose.

'Tis not in this life vouchsafed us
  All our way to see before;
Clears the path as we go forward,
  Step by step, and nothing more.

Noble ones have gone before thee:
  Fear not, while thine eyes may greet,
Leading on, their faithful footprints;
  In them strive to set thy feet.

Wait not for the noonday brightness:
  Haste thee through the morning
      gray;
Lo, the eastern glow before thee,
  Broadening, brightening ray by ray!

Thus, the just one's day beginneth:
  First, the streak of dawn is given;
Earth sees but the early morning,
  Cloudless noon is found in heaven.

M. J. S.

146 *Call of the Age*

We are living, we are dwelling
  In a grand and awful time:
In an age on ages telling,
  To be living is sublime.

Will ye play, then, will ye dally
  With your music and your wine?
Up! it is the Almighty's rally:
  God's own arm hath need of thine.

On! let all the soul within you
  For the Truth's sake go abroad
Strike! let every nerve and sinew
  Tell on ages, tell for God.

A. C. Coxe

STOCKWELL   8s & 7s

147   *He careth for us*

Yes, for me, for me He careth,
  With a father's tender care;
Yes, with me, with me he shareth
  Every burden, every fear.

Yes, o'er me, o'er me he watcheth,
  Ceaseless watcheth, night and day;
Yes, e'en me, e'en me he snatcheth
  From the perils of the way.

Yes, in me abroad he sheddeth
  Joys unearthly, love and light;
And to cover me he spreadeth
  His paternal wing of might.

Yes, in me, in me he dwelleth;
  I in him, and he in me:
And my empty soul he filleth,
  Here and through eternity.

Bonar

148   *Hope above Doubt*

When the gladsome day declineth,
  And around us falls the night,
Still down through the darkness shineth
  Some fair star to tell of light.

Never is the dark so blinding
  But outgleams some feeble ray,
Ever our despair reminding
  That somewhere is brightest day.

Though we then, thro' shadow groping,
  Stumble on, we still may know —
And our doubting change to hoping —
  Only light can shadow throw.

So the night itself, that hideth
  From our eyes the sunny sky,
Tells us that the light abideth, —
  For the stars still shine on high.

M. J. S.

65

GREENVILLE 8s & 7s DOUBLE

149 *The Age-long Battle*

Up the pathway of the ages,
    From the dim land of the past,
Come the sounds of battle-shouting,
    Armor-clang, and bugle-blast;
For our human race has ever   [cloud,
    Marched through blood and under
Tearing swaddling-bands for Freedom
    From the vanquished tyrant's shroud.

And to-day the wide-winged armies
    Of the God who marshals all
Sweep the earth, and cross the spaces
    Where the distant star-beams fall;
For the order of this battle,
    Waged for universal right,
Grasps an age-long, age-wide progress
    Out of darkness up to light.

Standing here as this day's sentries,
    Set to watch our little time,
Let us hear the past and future
    Calling us to deeds sublime.

Children of heroic fathers,
    We the future's sires must be;
And the coming generations
    Look to us to make them free.

Let us hold our lines not only,—
    Hear the order to advance!
Grasp the shield of Faith not only,—
    Lift on high Truth's flaming lance!
Fight for every hope that's human,
    Fight to shatter every chain,
Fight till every man and woman
    Owneth heart and soul and brain.

By the Ancient's long endeavor,
    By the Honorable's fame,
By our race and by our country,
    By each high and noble name,
By the God of hosts who leads us,
    By the future's dawning light,
Swear to stand and swear to struggle
    Till earth's might shall mean its right!

M. J. S.

66

150 *Divine Love*

LOVE divine, all love excelling,
Joy of heaven to earth come down,
Fix in us thy humble dwelling,
All thy faithful mercies crown.
Father, thou art all compassion;
Pure, unbounded love thou art:
Visit us with thy salvation,
Enter every longing heart.

Breathe, oh! breathe thy loving spirit
Into every troubled breast;
Let us all in thee inherit,
Let us find thy promised rest.
Come, almighty to deliver!
Let us all thy life receive;
Graciously come down, and never,
Never more thy temples leave.

Wesley's Col.

151 *Waiting for Death*

ONLY waiting till the shadows
Are a little longer grown;
Only waiting till the glimmer
Of the day's last beam is flown;
Till the light of earth is faded
From the heart once full of day;
Till the stars of heaven are breaking
Through the twilight soft and gray.

Only waiting till the shadows
Are a little longer grown;
Only waiting till the glimmer
Of the day's last beam is flown.
Then, from out the gathered darkness,
Holy, deathless stars shall rise,
By whose light my soul shall gladly
Tread its pathway to the skies.

Frances L. Mace

152 *The Word of the Lord abideth forever*

GOD of ages and of nations!
  Every race and every time
Hath received thine inspirations,
  Glimpses of thy truth sublime.
Ever spirits, in rapt vision,
  Passed the heavenly veil within;
Ever hearts, bowed in contrition,
  Found salvation from their sin.

Reason's noble aspiration
  Truth in growing clearness saw;
Conscience spoke its condemnation,
  Or proclaimed the Eternal Law.
While thine inward revelations
  Told thy saints their prayers were
    heard,
Prophets to the guilty nations
  Spoke thine everlasting word.

Lord, that word abideth ever:
  Revelation is not sealed,
Answering unto man's endeavor,
  Truth and Right are still revealed.
That which came to ancient sages,—
  Greek, Barbarian, Roman, Jew,—
Written in the heart's deep pages,
  Shines to-day, forever new!
                    Samuel Longfellow

153   *Christmas*

Now THE joyful Christmas morning,
  Breaking o'er the world below,
Tells again the wondrous story
  Of the Christ-child long ago.
Hark! we hear again the chorus
  Echoing through the starry sky;
And we join the heavenly anthem,
  "Glory be to God on high!"

Out of every clime and people,
  Under every holy name,
Is the everlasting gospel
  Good and glad for aye the same:
So we, in our happy Christmas,
  Breathe the universal creed,
Clasping hands with distant ages
  In a brotherhood indeed.

Sing aloud, then, hearts and voices!
  Shout, O new world, free and strong!
Hail of Light the deathless triumph,
  Join the old world's birthday song,—
"Glory be to God the highest!
  Peace on earth, good will to men!"
'Twas the morning stars that pealed it,
  Let the world respond again!
                    Mrs. M. N. Meigs

AUTUMN   8s & 7s   DOUBLE

154   *A Creed*

I BELIEVE in Human Kindness
  Large amid the sons of men,
Nobler far in willing blindness
  Than in censure's keenest ken.
I believe in Self-Denial,
  And its secret throb of joy;
In the Love that lives through trial,
  Dying not, though death destroy.

I believe in dreams of Duty,
  Warning us to self-control,—
Foregleams of the glorious beauty
  That shall yet transform the soul;
I believe in Love renewing
  All that sin [e'er sweeps] away,
Leaven-like its work pursuing
  Night by night and day by day;

I believe in Love Eternal,
  Fixed in God's unchanging will,
That, beneath the deep infernal,
  Hath a depth that's deeper still
In its patience, its endurance
  To forbear and to retrieve,
In the large and full assurance
  Of its triumph,—I believe.
                        " Good Words "

155   *A Purpose in Life.*

LIVE for something! be not idle;
  Look about thee for employ;
Sit not down to useless dreaming,—
  Labor is the sweetest joy.
Folded hands are ever weary,
  Selfish hearts are never gay.
Life for thee hath many duties:
  Active be, then, while you may.

Scatter blessings in your pathway,—
  Gentle words and cheering smiles:
Better far than gold and silver
  Are their grief-dispelling wiles.
As the pleasant sunshine falleth
  Ever on the grateful earth,
So let sympathy and kindness
  Gladden well the darkened hearth.

Hearts that are oppressed and weary,
  Drop the tear of sympathy;
Whisper words of hope and comfort;
  Give, and thy reward shall be
Joy unto thy soul returning
  From this perfect fountain-head.
Freely, as thou freely givest,
  Shall the grateful light be shed.
                        Anon.

GREENVILLE 8s & 7s Double

156 *Coming of God's Kingdom*

How shall come thy kingdom holy,
  In which all the earth is blest,
That shall lift on high the lowly,
  And to weary souls give rest?
Not with trumpet call of legions
  Bursting through the upper sky,
Waking earth through all its regions
  With their heaven-descending cry:

Not with dash or sudden sally,
  Swooping down with rushing wing;
But as, creeping up a valley,
  Come the grasses in the spring:
First one blade and then another,
  Still advancing are they seen,
Rank on rank, each by its brother,
  Till each inch of ground is green.

Through the weary days of sowing,
  Burning sun, and drenching shower,
Day by day, so slowly growing,
  Comes the waited harvest hour.
So the kingdom cometh ever,
  Though it seem so far away;
Each bright thought and true endeavor
  Hastens on the blessed day.

M. J. S.

157 *Surrounding the Mercy Seat*

Far from mortal cares retreating,
  Sordid hopes and fond desires,
Here, our willing footsteps meeting,
  Every heart to heaven aspires.
From the fount of glory beaming,
  Light celestial cheers our eyes,
Mercy from above proclaiming
  Peace and pardon from the skies.

Who may share this great salvation
  Every pure and humble mind;
Every kindred, tongue, and nation
  From the dross of guilt refined.
Blessings all around bestowing,
  God withholds his care from none;
Grace and mercy ever flowing
  From the fountain of his throne.

Every stain of guilt abhorring,
  Firm and bold in virtue's cause;
Still thy providence adoring,
  Faithful subjects to thy laws,—
Lord, with favor still attend us,
  Bless us with thy wondrous love;
Thou, our sun and shield, defend us!
  All our hope is from above

J. Taylor

PILGRIM 8s & 7s DOUBLE

158 *" The Lord is in his Holy Temple "*

God is in his holy temple;
   Earthly thoughts, be silent now,
While with reverence we assemble
   And before his presence bow.
He is with us now and ever,
   When we call upon his name,
Aiding every good endeavor,
   Guiding every upward aim.

God is in his holy temple,—
   In the pure and holy mind,
In the reverent heart and simple,
   In the soul from sense refined.
Then, let every low emotion
   Banished far and silent be,
And our souls in pure devotion,
   Lord, be temples worthy thee!

Anon

159 *Battle*

Dost thou hear the bugle sounding,
   Calling thee to take the field?
'Tis a battle all are waging:
   Thou must fight or thou must yield.
'Tis the battle of the ages:
   No man may the gage refuse.
Fight on one side or the other,
   No man can decline to choose.

If from off the field thou fliest,
   Even thus thou art a foe:
Who for truth no sword uplifteth
   He for error strikes a blow.
He who bravely fights must conquer;
   None can e'er defeated be;
For, to soldiers in God's battles,
   Death itself is victory.

M. J. S.

71

160 *Love*

O Love, with thy sweet chains
Bind both my hand and heart!
Who knoweth not thy bonds
In freedom hath no part.

'Tis such a bond that holds
Each in its circling round
The suns and golden stars,
Without a jar or sound.

So bind the race of men
In harmony and love,
Till each his orbit fills
Like those that shine above.

Loving our brother thus,
O Father, it shall be
Our love shall higher reach,
And end in loving thee.

M. J. S.

161 *The Father of All*

Upon one land alone
Has shone the holy light,
And all the world beside
Been left to walk in night?

Are only Christian men
The children of the Lord,
And have none others heard
The true, life-giving word?

Is there one only name
In all the tribes of earth,
Through which the longing soul
May find its higher birth?

Nay, every land is thine;
All men thy children be;
And every name of truth
A star that leads to thee.

M. J. S.

WORK, FOR THE NIGHT IS COMING

7s & 6s   DOUBLE

162   *Work, for the Night is Coming*

WORK, for the night is coming;
  Work through the morning hours;
Work while the dew is sparkling;
  Work 'mid springing flowers;
Work when the day grows brighter;
  Work in the glowing sun;
Work, for the night is coming,
  When man's work is done.

Work, for the night is coming;
  Work through the sunny noon;
Fill brightest hours with labor,
  Rest comes sure and soon.

Give every flying minute
  Something to keep in store;
Work, for the night is coming,
  When man works no more.

Work, for the night is coming,
  Under the sunset skies;
While their bright tints are glowing,
  Work, for daylight flies.
Work till the last beam fadeth,
  Fadeth to shine no more;
Work while the night is darkening,
  When man's work is o'er.

73

MISSIONARY HYMN   7s & 6s

163   *Worship*

WHEN, on some strain of music,
Our thoughts are wafted high;
When, touched with tender pity,
Kind tear-drops dim the eye;
When thrilled by scenes of grandeur
Or moved to deeds of love,
Do we not give thee worship,
O God in heaven above?

For thou art all life's beauty,
And thou art all its good;
By thy tides are we lifted
To every lofty mood.
Whatever good is in us,
Whatever good we see,
And every high endeavor,
Are they not all for thee?

Be it the organ's pealing,
Be it some mountain high,
Be it the swell of ocean,
Or calm of star-lit sky;

Be it the grace of childhood
Or look of human love,
All love of good is worship
That lifts toward God above.

M. J. S.

164   *Light for All*

THE light pours down from heaven,
And enters where it may;
The eyes of all earth's children
Are cheered with one bright day.
So let the mind's true sunshine
Be spread o'er earth as free,
And fill men's waiting spirits
As the waters fill the sea.

Then, let each human spirit
Enjoy the vision bright:
The Truth which comes from heaven
Shall spread like heaven's own light,
Till earth becomes God's temple,
And every human heart
Shall join in one great service,
Each happy in his part.

Anon

74

165 *"Consider the Lilies"*

He hides within the lily
A strong and tender Care,
That wins the earth-born atoms
To glory of the air;
He weaves the shining garments
Unceasingly and still,
Along the quiet waters,
In niches of the hill.

We linger at the vigil
With him who bent the knee
To watch the old-time lilies
In distant Galilee;
And still the worship deepens
And quickens into new,
As, brightening down the ages,
God's secret thrilleth through.

O Toiler of the lily,
Thy touch is in the man!
No leaf that dawns to petal
But hints the angel-plan:
The flower-horizons open,
The blossom vaster shows;
We hear thy wide worlds echo,—
"See how the lily grows!"

Shy yearnings of the savage
Unfolding, thought by thought,
To holy lives are lifted,
To visions fair are wrought:
The races rise and cluster,
And evils fade and fall,
Till chaos blooms to beauty,
Thy purpose crowning all!

W. C. Gannett

166 *Evening*

The shadows fall so gently
Adown the evening sky,
And, one by one, so softly
The stars look out on high!

With quiet benediction,
That whispers, "All is best,"
The sky, like loving mother,
The tired earth soothes to rest.

And, through this outward quiet,
There comes an inward calm
That to the soul's distraction
Applies its healing balm.

The weary heart looks upward,
And sees God's stars at rest,
And hears his gentle whisper
Down falling, "All is best."

M. J. S.

167 *Good-night*

Good-night, we say at parting,—
A night of rest and peace,
A night that from day's labor
Brings all a sweet release.

And when earth's night of shadow
For us has passed away,
May each, in heaven's long morning,
Greet all with glad Good-day!

M. J. S.

WEBB 7s & 6s

168 *Dedication of a Church*

O GOD, the stars of splendor
  Are thine eternal throne;
What to thee can we render
  That is not now thine own?
The earth, with all its wonder
  Of stone and wood and gem,
All things the wide sky under,—
  Thou hast created them.

Behold what we have builded,
  A temple to thy praise!
But 'tis thy wealth has gilded
  The walls thy power did raise.
Thine are its strength and beauty;
  For in thy might it stands
To speak of love and duty,
  Pure hearts and helping hands.

How shall we consecrate it,
  And make it truly thine,
That naught may separate it
  From all that is divine?
By seeking here forever
  To find thy truth; and then,
By one life-long endeavor,
  To help our fellow-men.

M. J. S.

169 *One Fold and One Shepherd*

Now is the time approaching,
  By prophets long foretold,
When all shall dwell together,
  One Shepherd and one fold.
Now, Jew and Gentile, meeting
  From many a distant shore,
Around one altar kneeling,
  One common Lord adore.

Let all that now divides us
  Remove and pass away,
Like shadows of the morning
  Before the blaze of day.
Let all that now unites us
  More sweet and lasting prove,
A closer bond of union
  In a blest land of love.

O long-expected dawning,
  Come with thy cheering ray:
Then shall the morning brighten,
  The shadows flee away!
O sweet anticipation!
  It cheers the watchers on
To pray and hope and labor
  Till the dark night be gone.

Jane Borthwick

170 *Safety in God*

God is my strong salvation;
  What foe have I to fear?
In darkness and temptation,
  My Light, my Help is near.
Though hosts encamp around me,
  Firm in the fight I stand;
What terror can confound me
  With God at my right hand?

Place on the Lord reliance;
  My soul, with courage wait:
His truth be thine affiance
  When faint and desolate.
His might thy heart shall strengthen,
  His love thy joy increase;
Mercy thy days shall lengthen,—
  The Lord will give thee peace.
                                    Montgomery

171 *To Truth*

O star of Truth, down shining
  Through clouds of doubt and fear,
I ask but 'neath your guidance
  My pathway may appear.
However long the journey,
  How hard soe'er it be,
Though I be lone and weary,
  Lead on, I'll follow thee!

I know thy blessed radiance
  Can never lead astray,
However ancient custom
  May tread some other way.
E'en if through untrod deserts,
  Or over trackless sea,
Though I be lone and weary,
  Lead on, I'll follow thee!

The bleeding feet of martyrs
  Thy toilsome road have trod;
But fires of human passion
  May light the way to God.
Then, though my feet should falter,
  While I thy beams can see,
Though I be lone and weary,
  Lead on, I'll follow thee!

Though loving friends forsake me,
  Or plead with me in tears;
Though angry foes may threaten,
  To shake my soul with fears;
Still to my high allegiance
  I must not faithless be:
Through life or death, forever
  Lead on, I'll follow thee!
                                    M. J. S.

172 *Trust and Wait*

Misfortune's hand hangs o'er me,
  My load of grief is great;
The path is rough before me,—
  Be patient, trust and wait.

The night is dark above me,
  Dawn breaks not, though 'tis late;
No heart awakes to love me,—
  Be patient, trust and wait.

Whatever ill betide thee,
  Though hopeless seem thy fate,
In high faith still abide thee,—
  Be patient, trust and wait.

What though the clouds be o'er thee,
  Nor storms their force abate?
His love still goes before thee,—
  Be patient, trust and wait.
                                    M. J. S.

77

173   *Rise, my Soul*

RISE, my soul, and stretch thy wings,
  Thy better portion trace;
Rise from transitory things
  Toward heaven, thy native place.
Sun and moon and stars decay,
  Time shall soon this earth remove:
Rise, my soul, and haste away
  To seats prepared above.

Rivers to the ocean run,
  Nor stay in all their course;
Fire ascending seeks the sun,—
  Both speed them to their source:
So a soul that's born of God
  Pants to view his glorious face,
Upward tends to his abode,
  To rest in his embrace.

Rippon's Coll.

174   *Quiet Religion*

OPEN, Lord, my inward ear,
  And bid my heart rejoice;
Bid my quiet spirit hear
  The comfort of thy voice.
Never in the whirlwind found,
  Or where earthquakes rock the place.
Still and silent is the sound,
  The whisper of thy grace.

From the world of sin and noise
  And hurry I withdraw;
For the small and inward voice
  I wait with humble awe:
Silent I am now and still,
  Dare not in thy presence move;
To my waiting soul reveal
  The secret of thy love.

Charles Wesley

78

WEBB 7s & 6s

175 *Jerusalem the Golden*

JERUSALEM the golden,
  With milk and honey blest!
Beneath thy contemplation
  Sink heart and voice opprest.
I know not, oh, I know not
  What joys await us there,
What radiancy of glory,
  What bliss beyond compare!

They stand, those halls of Zion,
  All jubilant with song,
And bright with many an angel
  And all the martyr throng.
There is the throne of glory;
  And there, from care released,
The shout of them that triumph,
  The song of them that feast.

And they who, strong and faithful,
  Have conquered in the fight,
Forever and forever
  Are clad in robes of white.
O land that sees no sorrow!
  O state that fears no strife!
O royal land of flowers!
  O realm and home of life!
                          Bernard of Cluny.
                       Tr. John Mason Neale

176 *Ever with Me*

THOU'RT with me, O my Father,
  At early dawn of day:
It is thy glory brighteneth
  The upward streaming ray.
It calls me by its beauty
  To rise and worship thee:
I feel thy glorious presence,
  Thy face I may not see.

Thou'rt with me, O my Father,
  In changing scenes of life,
In loneliness of spirit,
  In weariness of strife;
My sufferings, my comforts,
  Alternate at thy will:
I trust thee, O my Father,—
  I trust thee, and am still.

Thou'rt with me, O my Father,
  In evening's darkening gloom:
When earth in night is shrouded,
  Thy presence fills my room.
The trembling stars bring tidings
  Of kindness from above:
I love thee, O my Father,
  And feel that thou art love.
                       Jane Euphemia Saxby

79

177 *Nearer, my God, to Thee*

NEARER, my God, to thee,
Nearer to thee:
Even though it be a cross
That raiseth me,
||: Nearer, my God, to thee, :||
Nearer to thee.

Though like a wanderer,
Daylight all gone,
Darkness be over me,
My rest a stone,
Yet in my dreams I'd be
||: Nearer, my God, to thee, :||
Nearer to thee.

There let the way appear
Steps up to heaven;
All that thou sendest me
In mercy given;

Angels to beckon me
||: Nearer, my God, to thee, :||
Nearer to thee.

Then with my waking thoughts,
Bright with thy praise,
Out of my stony griefs
Bethel I'll raise:
So by my woes to be
||: Nearer, my God, to thee :||
Nearer to thee.

Or if on joyful wing,
Cleaving the sky,
Sun, moon, and stars forgot,
Upward I fly,—
Still all my song shall be,
||: Nearer, my God, to thee, :||
Nearer to thee.

S. F. Adams

178 *National Hymn*

My country, 'tis of thee,
Sweet land of liberty,—
Of thee I sing:
Land where my fathers died,
Land of the pilgrim's pride,
From every mountain side
Let freedom ring!

My native country, thee,—
Land of the noble free,—
Thy name I love:
I love thy rocks and rills,
Thy woods and templed hills;
My heart with rapture thrills
Like that above.

Let music swell the breeze,
And ring from all the trees
Sweet freedom's song!
Let mortal tongues awake;
Let all that breathe partake;
Let rocks their silence break,—
The sound prolong!

Our fathers' God, to thee,
Author of liberty,—
To thee we sing:
Long may our land be bright
With freedom's holy light;
Protect us by thy might,
Great God, our King!

S. F. Smith

179 *" God save the State "*

God bless our native land!
Firm may she ever stand
Through storm and night!
When the wild tempests rave,
Ruler of winds and wave,
Do thou our country save
By thy great might.

For her our prayer shall rise
To God, above the skies;
On him we wait:
Thou who art ever nigh,
Guarding with watchful eye,
To thee aloud we cry,
God save the State!

J. S. Dwight

180 *Rest*

Like travellers that stray
Through countries far away,
  But long for home ;
Like birds that seek their nest,
Like child to mother's breast,
Weary for peace and rest,
  To thee we come.

From our too anxious thought,
From all our hands have wrought,
  From truth's long quest ;
From danger's wild alarms,
From evil's fatal charms,
To thine embracing arms,
  We fly for rest.

As ships their anchors cast
When all the storms are past,
  Their troubles o'er ;
Whatever may betide,
Here, sheltered by thy side,
In safety we'll abide
  Forever more !

M. J. S.

181 *Prayer*

Here on this little world,
Through cloud and sunshine whirled
  Athwart the sky,
We look out on the light,
We look up through the night,
And wonder if God's might
  May hear our cry.

Is all a heartless void,
Worlds made and worlds destroyed,
  With none to care?
Or somewhere in the deep
Is One who does not sleep,
But wakes to watch and keep,
  And note our prayer?

We trust no joy or pain
Is ever felt in vain,—
  That not one cry
Dies on the empty air ;
No human heart's despair
Shall miss the loving care
  That rules on high.

M. J. S.

BETHANY   6s & 4s

182   *The Undying Things*

Kind words can never die,
  Cherished and blest:
God knows how deep they lie
  Stored in the breast.
Like childhood's simple rhymes,
Said o'er a thousand times,
And in all years and climes,
  They cannot die.

Sweet thoughts can never die,
  Though, like the flowers,
Their brightest hues may fly
  In wintry hours;
But, when the gentle dew
Gives them their charms anew,
With many an added hue
  They bloom again.

Childhood can never die:
  Thoughts of the past
Float in the memory,
  Bright to the last.
Many a happy thing,
Many a sunny spring,
Come on time's ceaseless wing
  Back to the heart.

The soul can never die,
  Though in the tomb
Our mortal bodies lie,
  Wrapt in its gloom.
What though the flesh decay?
The soul will pass away,
And live in endless day
  With God above.

83

183 *God our Shepherd*

The Lord is my Shepherd, no want shall
    I know:
I feed in green pastures, safe folded I
    rest;
He leadeth my soul where the still
    waters flow,
Restores me when wandering, redeems
    when oppressed.

Through the valley and shadow of
    death though I stray,
Since thou art my guardian, no evil I
    fear:
Thy rod shall defend me, thy staff be
    my stay;
No harm can befall, with my comforter
    near.

In the midst of affliction, my table is
    spread;
With blessings unmeasured my cup run-
    neth o'er;
With perfume and oil thou anointest
    my head:
Oh! what shall I ask of thy providence
    more?

Let goodness and mercy, my bountiful
    God,
Still follow my steps till I meet thee
    above:
I seek by the path which my forefathers
    trod
Through the land of their sojourn, thy
    kingdom of love.

Montgomery

84

184   *For Divine Strength*

FATHER, in thy mysterious presence
kneeling,
Fain would our souls feel all thy
kindling love;   [revealing
For we are weak, and need some deep
Of trust and strength and calmness
from above.

Lord, we have wandered forth through
doubt and sorrow,
And thou hast made each step an
onward one;   [morrow,—
And we will ever trust each unknown
Thou wilt sustain us till its work is
done.

In the heart's depths, a peace serene and
holy
Abides; and when pain seems to have
its will,   [slowly,
Or we despair, oh, may that peace rise
Stronger than agony, and we be still!

Now, Father, now, in thy dear presence
kneeling,   [love;
Our spirits yearn to feel thy kindling
Now make us strong: we need thy deep
revealing   [from above.
Of trust and strength and calmness

S. Johnson

185   *"Who by searching can find out God"*

I CANNOT find thee. Still on restless
pinion
My spirit beats the void where thou
dost dwell;
I wander lost through all thy vast dominion,
And shrink beneath thy light ineffable.

I cannot find thee. Even when, most
adoring,   [prayer,
Before thy shrine I bend in lowliest
Beyond these bounds of thought, my
thought upsoaring
From furthest quest comes back:
thou art not there.

Yet high above the limits of my seeing,
And folded far within the inmost
heart,   [being,
And deep below the deeps of conscious
Thy splendor shineth: there, O God,
thou art.

I cannot lose thee. Still in thee abiding,
The end is clear, how wide soe'er I
roam;   [is guiding,
The law that holds the worlds my steps
And I must rest at last in thee, my
home.

Eliza Scudder

SENTENCE.

BASS SOLO AND QUARTET

HOWARD M. DOW.

Maestoso.

The Lord is in His ho - ly tem - ple! Let all the earth . . keep si-lence!

The Lord is in His ho - ly tem - ple! Let all the earth, . the earth keep silence!

The Lord is in His ho - ly tem - ple, Let all the earth . . keep

si - lence be - fore him! A - - - men! A - men! A - - - - - men!

187 THE VOICE OF THE PAST.

Words by M. J. SAVAGE
Allegretto.
Music by HOWARD M. DOW.

1 Comrades, hark! the air a-bout us, Emp-ty as it all ap-pears, Thrills and pul-ses with the e-choes Of the long de-part-ed years. There are foot-steps all a-round us; Long the an-cient drum-beat rolls; Voi-ces call from out the con-flict Of the "times that tried men's souls."

2 We are athletes in th' arena:
Round us rising, tier on tier,
Shadowy legions of the Fathers,
"Clouds of witnesses," appear.
And they cheer the vigorous onset
With a proud and glad acclaim,
But for him who shirks his duty
Tears have they of wrath and shame.

3 Listen! for the deathless voices
Of that Century-distant day
Shape themselves to one clear echo,
Ringing out above the fray,—
"Sons, be worthy of the Fathers!
They were men who dared to stake
Life and fortune and fair honor
For their periled freedom's sake.

4 "Dare be loyal unto duty;
Barter not your soul for gain;
Trade not principle for party;
Seek the highest truth t'attain.
While to truth you are but faithful
Shun not e'en alone to stand;
One, with God, shall still be victor,
And th' Omnipotent command.

5 "When you've fought the human battle,
Given to every one his right,—
There shall come an end of struggle,
And the darkness shall be light.
Clang of arms, and strife of brothers,
And the flow of blood shall cease;
Swords be beaten into plow-shares,
And the weary earth have peace."

87

SOLO & QUARTET.

(By permission of White, Smith & Co.)

Written by M. J. SAVAGE.   Music by HOWARD M. DOW.

Allegretto.

p Soprano Solo.

1. In the hor-ror of the darkness of the old pri-me-val night, Men

Ped.

crouched in caves and shadows, trembling praying for the light: And they shouted in their gladness when the

Sun rose warm and bright, And day came marching on! In the long and dreary winters when the

8va........................
Ped.

earth was cold and dead, When the ice was in the valleys, and the wild sky overhead. How the

Quartet 1st verse

freezing people shouted when the cru - el winter fled, And Spring came marching on !

8va..

QUARTETTE.

1. Hail   with Joy the blessed Spring-time ! Hail   with Joy the blessed Spring-time !

2. Hope shall triumph o - ver doubt-ing ! Hope shall triumph o - ver doubt - ing !

3. Day shall reign o'er night forev - er ! Life shall conquer death forev - er !

Hail   with Joy the bless-ed Spring - time ! When win - ter flees a - way.

Hope shall tri-umph o - ver doubt - ing ! And clouds shall drift a - way.

Joy shall ban - ish grief for - ev - - - er ! And God shall rule for aye !

Tenor Solo.

2. Birth of day and birth of spring-time! Dawning light and opening flow'rs! Right

Ped.

well has mankind worshipped Easter, best of heavenly Pow'rs! Of light and life the symbol, vanquished

death and happy hours, While Spring is marching on! So when their hearts were heavy with the

8va.
Ped.

91

EASTER SONG.

tho'ts of death and doom, In that old wondrous story of the rock-hewn, empty tomb, Men

read the mighty triumph o-ver death of life and bloom, And hope went march-ing on !

(Quartet 2nd verse.)

Soprano Solo.

3. Whether fact, or whether fai - ry-tale, the hu - man heart that grieves O - ver

92

dear ones that departed with the fall-ing of the leaves; So   long as love remaineth sweet, so

long it still believes That life is marching on!   So   hail thee, blessed Easter! Sign of

im-mor-tal - i - ty! Night fears thee, winter flees thee, and death himself shall die,   While

EASTER SONG.

(Quartet 3rd. verse.)

light, and life, and happi-ness, shall follow thee on high,   As thou art march-ing on!

8va.
Ped.

CHRISTMAS CAROL.

189

Words by M. J. SAVAGE.

Music by HOWARD M. DOW.

Allegretto.

SOLO.

1. In the old time, runs the sto - ry,   There was once . . a won-drous
2. Since that day the chil - dren's voi - ces   Have caught up . . the glad re-
3. Each new child's a new Mes - si - ah,   Wheth - er cot . . or pal - ace

94

night,   When from out the   un - seen glo - ry Burst a song of glad de -
frain ;   And to - night the   heart re - joic - es That the hour comes round a -
born,   Lead-ing on the   race still high -er Toward the glad redemp-tion

light ;   It was when the   stars were gleaming, Shepherds watched their flocks, and
gain ;   And the chil - dren are our an-gels; With one loud   acclaim they
morn ;   Each new child's   a word new spoken, God to earth   come down a-

then   In their wak-ing   or their dreaming, Angels sang, "Good-will to men." !
cry,   Answ'ring back the   glad e - van-gel's "Glory be to God on   high." !
gain   With his prom-ise   nev-er bro - ken, "Peace on earth, good-will to men." !

CHORUS.

Mer - ry Christmas! Mer-ry Christmas! Let us make the heavens ring! Ech-o

Mer - ry Christmas! Mer-ry Christmas! Let us make the heavens ring! Ech-o

back the an - gel's mes - sage, With the songs the chil - dren sing! . . . .

back the an - gel's mes - sage, With the songs the chil - dren sing! . . . .

CHRISTMAS SONG.

Words by M. J. SAVAGE.

Music by HOWARD M. DOW.

*The Solo may be played either by Cornet or Swell Trumpet as desired.

97

cres - - cen - - -

cres - - cen - - -

do. *f*

do. *f*

CHRISTMAS SONG.

ritard.

ff   *dimin.*

ritard.

ritard.

ff   *dimin.*   *p* *pp*

Cornet obligato.
Andantino. *p*

Soprano Solo. *mf*

1. Born at last! the great Messi - ah Bringeth in the bet-ter
3. The op-press - or rides in tri - umph, And the weak are in the

day.   Peace on earth, good will from heaven,   Lo! the star   that leads the
dust.   Shall the e - - vil always prosper?   Is   it   vain   the hope we

way!   So runs on   the ancient sto - ry   Of the shepherds, that strange
trust? Peace comes not,   but ev - er strug - gle,   Man his broth - er fighteth

night,   How   they   heard   the quir - ing an - - gels, And be-
still,   In   the   yet   far dis - tant fu - - ture Lies the

ritard. ff colla voce.

held   the wondrous light,   And be-held the won-drous light.
bright   land of good will,   Lies the bright land of good will.

101

QUARTET.
Soprano.

Alto.
2. But the wea - ry world still waiteth, And the prom - ise long de-lays; Still the

Tenor.

Bass.

Organ, ad lib.

hope - star lead-eth on-ward O - ver dark and drea - ry ways. Oft the

Star   it-self shines dimly, From a sky, that clouds obscure: And the heavens lose their

pi - - ty For the cry - - ing of the poor, For the crying of the poor.

Soprano solo D.S.
(3d Verse.)

103

CHRISTMAS SONG.

CHRISTMAS SONG.

a - - ges   Comes to   birth   the perfect right.   Nev - er

done,   but al - ways grow   -   ing,   God un - folds   his mighty

CHRISTMAS SONG.

106

CHRISTMAS HYMN.

Written by M. J. SAVAGE.

Music by HOWARD M. DOW.

1. Let the heavens break forth in sing-ing! Stars, that saw the bright earth born,
2. Earth, so long the home of sor-row, Sweeping on thro' clouds and night,

Her - ald forth the sun that's bringing To the world its glad-dest morn!
Hail with loud ac - claim the morrow! For it brings a fair - er light.

Heav'n-ly glo - ry, heav'n-ly beau-ty, Crown the earth this Christmas morn.
Bright the present, bright the fut-ure Glow beneath this Christmas morn.

3 Angels that excel in glory,
Elder brothers of the sky,
Help us sing the lofty story
Of divine humanity.
"God is with us, God is with us,"
Speaks this blessed Christmas morn.

4 Heaven and earth, and men and Angels,
Lift one voice in glad acclaim,
And on high o'er all Evangels,
Shout aloud the Christmas name!
Earth and Heaven. Earth and Heaven,
Are at one this Christmas morn.

192 CHRISTMAS CAROL.

Words by M. J. SAVAGE.

Music by HOWARD M. DOW.

p Solo   p

1. O shep-herds, shepherds, did you hear From out the night-sky ring - ing, Be-
2. O chil - dren, we can nev - er tell Were we a - wake or dreaming; There
3. O shep-herds! chil-dren! in your souls, If you will on - ly hear it, The

Allegretto moderato.

mf

neath the stars, or far, or near, The sound of voi - ces sing - ing? And
was on us a ho - ly spell, Our hearts from fear re-deem - ing. But
an - gel's song for - ev - er rolls, The mu - sic of your spir - it. Care

mf

did you see the an - gels nigh, Or just as they were go - ing, Catch
wheth - er in our hearts the song, Or in the air a - bove us, Its
not to hear with out-ward ear, Be false to du - ty nev - er; The

glimps - es of them in the sky, Them by their brightness know - ing?
ho - ly notes will ech - o long, And teach that God doth love us.
in - ward song you'll al-ways hear, "Good - will to men for - ev - er."

CHRISTMAS CAROL.

QUARTET.

Soprano.

1. For could we once but see them near, Or know that they were by us, We

Contralto.

2. Be sure that God is ev - er near, He is for - ev - er by you; Do

Tenor.

3. Yes! be you sure He's ev - er near, God is for - ev - er by you; Do

Bass.

then should nev - er know a fear, And sor - row,—it would fly us.

right— and nev - er know a fear, And sor - row,—it will fly you.

right— and you will know no fear, And sor - row,—it will fly you.

109

NATIONAL HYMN.

Words by M. J. SAVAGE.

Music by HOWARD M. DOW.

Andante.

1. Our fa - thers' God, who still The chil-dren's God wilt be, With

lov - ing thank - ful - ness We come to wor - ship Thee;

The songs of praise our sires have sung Shall e - cho still up - on our tongue.

2

A hundred years ago
They saw in vision bright
A nation that should know,
And knowing, do the right;
Where all the people should be free
To rule themselves and worship Thee.

3

They spared nor blood nor tears
To make the vision true.
May we in coming years
Their glorious work renew!
And thus the dream shall grow to be
A fair, world-wide reality.

4

And when our hands have raised
This temple of the free,
In it shalt Thou be praised,
And Thine the glory be:
For Thine the thought, and Thine the might
That 'lift the ages into light.

194   PRAYER FOR PEACE.

Words by M. J. SAVAGE.

Music adapted from MORNINGTON.

Adagio.

1. { When the bur - - dens on . . . . us press, }
   { Of . . the sad . . world's wea - - - ri - ness, }
Then, O

Lord, May Thy peace our long - - - ing bless.   A - men!

Ending.

2
When the sun withdraws its light,
And our day is quenched in night,
    Then, O Lord,
May the stars of hope be bright.

3
When on life's tempestuous sea,
Our frail bark drifts hopelessly,
    Then, O Lord,
Wilt Thou our safe harbor be?

195   THE AMERICAN SONG.

Words by M. J. SAVAGE.

Music by V. CIRILLO.

Allegro marziale.

111

THE AMERICAN SONG.

SOLO.
Allegro marziale.   *espressivo.*

1. What
2. From the

Allegro marziale.

rail.   *sf*   *p*

song shall A-mer - i   ca sing,   Young heir   of   the el - der
dark low - lands   of the past,   Swelling loud o'er the vic - tim's

world,   Whose knee   ne'er bent   to   a   ty - rant   king, Whose
cries,   The he - ro's   shout   sweeps up   the   blast! Where

p   *f*

112

ban - ner de-feat ne'er furled? A song for the brave and the
wound - ed free - dom dies. The drum's dull beat and the

free ! No ech - o of ancient rhyme ; But a shout of
trumpet's blare From the far - off years are heard ; But the pæan of

hope for the day to be, The light of the com - ing
kings is mans des - pair And the hope of the world de-

113

CHORUS.

Soprano.
Marziale.

A song for the brave and the free! No
The drum's dull beat and the trum-pet's blare From th;

Alto.

Tenor.

time!
ferred.

A song for the brave and the
The drum's dull beat, and the

ech - - o of ancient rhyme; But a shout f
far - off years are heard; But the pæan of

free! No ech - - o of ancient rhyme; But a
trum-pet's blare, From the far - off years are heard; But the

114

hope for the day to be, The light of the coming
kings is man's des - pair And the hope of the world de-

shout of hope for the day to be, The light of the com-ing
pæan of kings is man's des - pair And the hope of the world de-

time! The light of the com - - ing time.
ferred, The hope of the world de - - - ferred.

3 'Tis the song of the free we sing!
 Of a good time not yet born,
 Where each man of himself is King;
 Of a day whose gladsome morn
 Shall see the earth beneath our feet
 And a fair sky overhead;
 When those now sad shall find life sweet,
 And none shall hunger for bread.
  CHO.—Shall see the earth, etc.

4 Sing then our American Song!
 'Tis no boast of triumphs won
 At the price of another's wrong,
 Or of foul deeds foully done.
 We fight for the wide world's right,
 To enlarge life's scope and plan,
 To flood the earth with hope and light,
 To build the kingdom of man!
  CHO.—We fight for the etc.

www.ingramcontent.com/pod-product-compliance
Lightning Source LLC
Chambersburg PA
CBHW030618270326
41927CB00007B/1230